Memories of Dziadka:
Rural life in the Kingdom of Poland 1880-1912 and Immigration to America

By Stephen Szabados

Copyright © 2014 Stephen Szabados

All rights reserved.

ISBN: **150080309X**
ISBN-13: **978-1500803094**

DEDICATION

To my grandfather Stefan John Zuchowski

TABLE OF CONTENTS

	Acknowledgments	i
	Introduction	1
1	Farm Land in Dmochy Poland	5
2	The Zuchowski Family and Rural Life	13
3	Polish Holidays and Customs	33
4	Reasons to Emigrate	47
5	Emigration and Voyage	53
6	Arrival in America	67
7	Life in America	79
8	Conclusion: What does it all mean	101
	Glossary	109
	Endnotes	111
	Bibliography	117
	Index	121

ACKNOWLEDGMENTS

Most of the information for this book is based on information that I found for my grandfather in documents, stories that he told me and from my memories of him when we lived with him. However, to tell the complete story of a Polish immigrant, I used information from many other resources.

I owe a special thanks to my cousin Pawel Zawistowski who supplied me with details of life in Dmochy Kudly as experienced by his mother Cecylia. My son's father-in-law Glenn Sittig gave me some very interesting insights into his life while growing up on a farm. Craig Pfannkuche who is a wealth of knowledge deserves my thanks for help finding the train schedules that aided me in recreating my grandfather's train trip from Philadelphia to Bloomington, Illinois. Joan Huff, my good friend and fellow genealogy volunteer at the Arlington Heights Memorial Library helped one more time with her proofing and editing skills.

Once again my wife Susan and my family were patient with me as I sat writing and editing my manuscript. My friends in genealogy were also very patient as I described the book to them so I could form some of my ideas.

Thank you all.

Memories of Dziadka

INTRODUCTION TO DZIADKA

This book is about the life of a Polish immigrant from the Russian partition of Poland. I describe the main character as my grandfather but this can be the story of many of the Polish immigrants who arrived in America in the early 1900s.

The book begins with the description of the area where my grandfather was born. It continues with an account of his activities that he experienced during his early life in rural Polish Russia. The third chapter describes the customs and traditions that his family celebrated as he grew to manhood. Chapter Four discusses the possible reasons for his decision to leave his family and the land of his birth. Chapter Five describes his trek across Poland and Germany to the port of Bremerhaven, his experience in the port and his voyage across the North Atlantic Ocean. The next chapter discusses his arrival in America and the process for admittance to the United States after leaving the ship. This chapter also describes his train trip from Philadelphia to Bloomington, Illinois. Chapter Seven details his life in America.

My goal is to share the stories of the lives of Polish immigrants to make it easy for other people to read and understand the hardships these brave people endured. Most readers know the stories covering their immigration and their lives in America and my hope is to add more understanding of the daily lives of the Polish people living in the rural areas of Poland and the sacrifices that occurred boarded the ships. I use my grandfather as the central figure in this book but this is not his biography. I use details of my grandfather's life but add accounts of other people to tell a complete life story. My grandfather was not a person whose accomplishments you would normally find in history books. However, his life is an

Memories of Dziadka

example of a typical Polish immigrant in the early 1900s. I chose to tie all of the stories and information to one person to make this a more interesting story. I felt this method would be easier to show the impact of various facets on someone's life.

When writing your family history, remember to "put some meat on the bones of your ancestors." They were more than the names and dates on the documents. Use the pictures in the family albums. Save and label these precious photos. Find stories that tell how they interacted with their neighbors, friends and family. Include information about social history and the events that may have impacted their lives. Ask yourself what their lives were like and find accounts that will explain their actions.

I find that family history is not just the collection of names, pictures, charts and documents. I use summaries to help organize my research. These pages act as quick reference sheets and allow me to find information faster. At first my summaries are lists of facts but as they grow, I begin to see stories coming out of the information that I find. My summaries allow me to see my ancestors come alive. They were human beings who interacted with the people and were affected by the events around them. Each document that lists them is a snap shot of their lives and I find that each detail should be captured and analyzed. All of these are related and a written family history should show their relationships between the facts and the people. I try to envision how each fact might impact their lives.

My grandfather was a big man. At least he seemed that way to me when I was young. He was actually 6 feet tall and about 210 pounds. My earliest memory of him was that he was always at home and did not work. I normally found him sitting on the front porch watching over the neighborhood. When the weather was bad, he sat in his rocker in the living room and watched TV. I found out later that he had suffered a number of strokes starting in 1949 and these prevented him from returning to work at the railroad shops. He and my grandmother lived off his disability pension that he received from the Railroad Retirement Administration.

Introduction

During the 1950s, grandpa, grandma, uncle, my parents, my sister and I lived in my grandparents' house on West Mulberry Street in Bloomington, Illinois. This was a time that gave me the opportunity to ask my grandfather about his life in Poland. However, he was a quiet man and talked very little. I did have some interest in learning more about my Polish roots and I did ask him questions about his life in Poland. However, he was reluctant to describe this part of his life. My persistence did yield some details but fifty years later when I began my genealogy research in earnest, he was no longer with us and I wish I had gotten more from him.

The foundation for this book is based on the details that I have found about my grandfather in documents such as his military papers, passenger manifests, census records, railroad retirement papers and land transactions. I also included the oral history that was told to me and my descriptions of the many aspects of his life that I saw myself because we lived with him or next door for 15 years.

My research encouraged me to seek out other resources to add more details to my family history about my grandfather. I found some of these details in accounts written by other researchers about their ancestors or in books dealing with other aspects of Polish life or Polish history. As I did my genealogy research, I took special interest of any accounts on Polish life. Any stories of life in Polish Russia were of special interest to me and I took more time to study the information and take notes.

Here are a few of the books that I found helpful:
- The two volumes of *God's Playground* by Norman Davies are an excellent history of Poland. Davies gives many details from archival papers that gave me new insights of events that affected my ancestors.
- Another great reference was the book *Polish Customs, Traditions and Folklore* by Sophie Hodorowicz Knab which gave many details about Polish life that was helpful in

visualizing my grandfather's early years.
- Some of the early pages of the book *Polish Immigrants and Industrial Chicago* by Dominic A Pacyga gave some excellent details of the difficulties that immigrants had in crossing the German border and the challenges they faced once they arrived.
- Many books have been written describing how immigrants enter through Ellis Island but the book *Forgotten Doors, the Other Ports of Entry to the United States* edited by M. Mark Stolarik gives many details of the challenges faced by immigrants arriving through other U.S. cities. I used this book to help describe the experience that my grandfather had as he passed through the port at Philadelphia.

Another important source that I used were my cousins Pawel Zawistowski and Darius Tolcyzk who were born in Poland and whose ancestors were born in the same village as my grandfather. The stories from their parents and grandparents filled in many of the details of life in my grandfather's village.

My book is about a simple, uneducated man who had noble ancestors but could not inherit anything in Poland. It is a story about a strong, young man who joined the thousands of Polish immigrants on their journey to the United States to find better opportunities. It describes his early life in Poland; it discusses possible reasons for his emigration; it describes what he endured in his journey to America and finally it describes his new life in America.

Hopefully you will find many of the details of my grandfather's life were similar to your ancestors. These could be clues that lead you to the documents and stories about your heritage.

CHAPTER ONE: FARM LAND IN DMOCHY POLAND

Grandpa's birthplace
My grandfather Stefan Jan Zuchowski was born in the farming area of Dmochy Poland in 1893. His parents were Leopold Zuchowski and Anna Dmochowska. Baptismal records indicated that their ancestors were of noble birth (urodzony).

The small village where Stefan was born was called Dmochy Kudly and it had only two other families living there when he was born. Both of these families were cousins of Stefan's mother Anna. The common ancestor for the three families was born in about 1730.

Fields and homes near Dmochy Kudly (circa 1890)
Note that the houses in the background all have thatched roofs

Dmochy Kudly was located about 50 miles northeast of Warsaw. Today, the village name of Dmochy Kudly no longer appears on modern maps but the homes are still there. The village was merged with the adjoining village of Dmochy Mrozy in the late 1990s to streamline the county's administration. The Catholic Church where Stefan was baptized was in Czyzew which was located four miles (6 km) south of Dmochy Kudly.

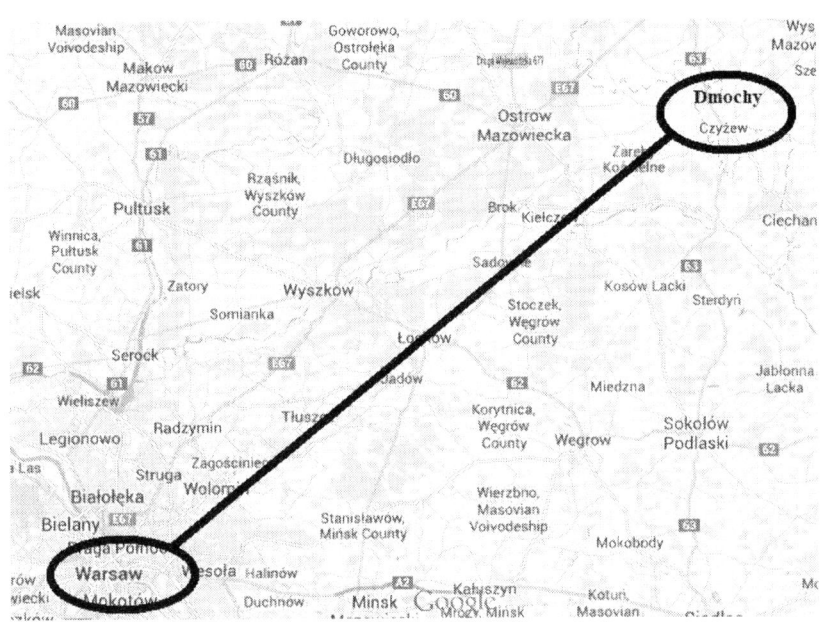

In the Dmochy, there were many forests but the inhabitants cleared large sections of tilled fields used for farming and the area also included meadows and fields that were used as pastures for dairy cows. Farming in the area was important but difficult due to the poor soil, harsh winter temperatures and a short growing season.

Some of the larger villages developed cottage industries such as textiles in the 1800s. In 1854, the railroad line between Petersburg and Warsaw was completed with the railroad tracks being located on the south edge of Czyzew. This allowed for the expansion of the cottage industries in Dmochy with the export of their goods to the large cities of Warsaw and St Petersburg. The manufacture of the Jewish Orthodox tsitses in Czyzew developed into an important industry because of their excellent quality. They were in high demand by Russian Jews and they were exported to America. However, the economy of the Dmochy area remained dependant on its agricultural products and the area did not attract large investment in manufacturing operations.

Dmochy Kudly was one of many small villages that had a two-part name with Dmochy as the first part of their name and was followed by a second name. All of these villages were once part of the large manor estate called Dmochy. The *Slownik Geograficzny* which was published in 15 volumes between 1881 and 1900 described Dmochy as an "okolica szlachecka" or a noble-owned settlement. This gazetteer listed eleven villages that had Dmochy in their name.

Today the people of the villages of Dmochy Kudly, Dmochy Wochy and Dmochy Mrozy are very proud at being from "szlachta" and not from peasants. Parents did not allow their children to socialize with the children from the villages that were for the workers. Although this is not true today, some parents followed this practiced into the 1950s and 1960s. Marriages between szlachta and peasants were also frown upon and difficult to arrange.

The family of the Polish noble who owned the Dmochy manor farm took the surname of Dmochowski. The noble had been given dominion over these lands by the ruler of Poland in order to recruit settlers who would develop the lands for more income and create a buffer on the frontier that would help protect against invasions from the east.

From 1223 to 1700, the Mongols and Tatars invaded the lands of Russia, Hungary, Lithuania and Poland almost annually to plunder and capture slaves. The Mongols invaded Poland three times in the 13th century and killed many people and destroyed much of the land. In 1506, Poland was invaded by Tatars from the Crimean Khanate who had an army of 10,000 men. Poland eventually defeated and drove the Tatars back. Tatar forces invaded again in

Memories of Dziadka

1589, invading Lwów and Tarnopol, but were beaten back by Cossack forces. After 1599 the Polish-Lithuanian Commonwealth suffered a series of Tatar invasions, the goal of which was to loot, pillage and capture slaves.

The mid-1600s saw repeated invasions by Sweden and the borderland area to the southeast Poland was in a state of semi-permanent warfare until the 18th century. The Dmochy area was spared from the devastations from these invasions but its nobles had to supply forces to fight in the southeast lands.

The history of the Dmochy area starts in the early 1400s when the prince of Mazovia granted Przeclaw of Swiercze title to land in the northern territory of Poland. Przeclaw was granted the right to nobility and in return he was to attract settlers to defend the border against invasion and also to develop the lands generate income for the prince and Przeclaw. His new estate was given the name Dmoszywo by the prince and today Dmochy is the variant of this ancient name.

It should be noted that Przeclaw received his grant about the time when the border between Lithuania and Mazovia was finally established. The borderland between Lithuania and Mazovia had shifted from one government to the other several times over three centuries but was finally settled in about 1410.

With his grant, Przeclaw became a Polish Magnate or feudal lord who owned a large area of land. The estate was large and many villages were established with settlers who farmed the land and trained as soldiers to defend the land in time of invasion. Przeclaw wielded political influence and gained wealth from taxes and rents from his lands.

Przeclaw was one of many Polish knights who were granted lands from the Polish prince. The knights had been rewarded for their loyal service or were repaid for bravery in battle. The lands in their grants were usually along the frontier and the knights were to recruit settlers who would become soldiers and defend the frontier in time of war with Poland's neighbors or other invading armies such as the Mongols and the Crimean Tatars.

The nobles used their new lands to gain wealth because the new settlers paid the noble rents on the land where they lived and taxes on the crops produced on the lands.

Traditionally, members of the szlachta were owners of landed property. Their property was "manor farms" or *folwarks*. To be a member of the Polish szlachta gave the noble many privileges that were increased over time and made them different that feudal lords in other countries. Over the centuries, the Polish nobility negotiated substantial political and legal privileges that gave them more freedoms and power than most nobles were accustomed to. One major power was to elect their king and to vote on laws. Social status in Poland was determined by control of the land. This deterred the Polish magnates from developing commercial enterprises that were becoming a major factor in economic growth and power in the other major countries of Europe.

The agricultural economy that was prevalent in Poland as they entered into 1700s led to a weakening of the power of Poland compared to its neighbors and set the stage for the Partitions of Poland from 1772 to 1795. After the Partitions and until 1918, the legal status of the Polish nobility was essentially dependent upon the policies of the three partitioning powers: Prussia, Russia and Austria. Finally, the legal privileges of the szlachta were legally abolished during the Second Polish Republic in 1921.

The lands in the Russian controlled partition benefited from the Tsarist policy of developing industrial production in the Polish lands. Initially the growth of manufacturing in the cities absorbed the growing surplus of farm labor. Landless freed serfs and landless minor nobility flocked to the cities to find work to support their families. However this changed after the Russo-Japanese War in 1904. Their eastern markets were closed off and the Russian government began shifting its industrial production from factories in the Kingdom of Poland to historic Russian lands. This had to be a major factor in the sharp increase of Polish emigration at this time.

Memories of Dziadka

Over the centuries, the large estates of the Polish magnates also changed significantly. As the magnates died, their manor farms were sub-divided by their heirs into smaller and smaller parcels. During this time the lands were partible inheritances. Once the lands became too small to divide further the laws change to make inherited lands to be primogeniture or non-partible. Primogeniture inheritance limited the assets to be given only to the firstborn son.

The small villages that were associated with these smaller individual parcels came to be named after their new owners and usually had a two-part name. The first part of the name of the small settlement identified the original manor estate and second part was the name or nickname of its new owner. For my Grandpa's village, Kudly may refer to the owner having a heavy beard or being very hairy.

The *Slownik Geograficzny* listed that the Dmochy villages were relatively small with from 2 households and 8 people to 14 households and 83 people. Dmochy Kudly had 3 families and 21 residents; Dmochy Wochy had 12 households and 60 residents; Dmochy Mrozy had 7 households and 56 people.

The small farms could only support one family and they could not be sub-divided again. By the 1700s, the inheritance law was changed to have only the oldest son eligible to inherit the land. These farms were very small and the nobles who owned them were not wealthy. Often they lived like peasants and about the only thing that distinguished them from the peasants were that they had a title, a signet ring, and a sword.

The 1881 *Slownik Geograficzny* entry for Dmochy says the total population of the Dmochy district was 6,212, of whom 107 were "legitimate nobles," and 3,640 were "minor farming nobles" who were poor. There were also 1,033 peasants who owned land. So you see, the minor nobility, living in little settlements and working their small farms, outnumbered peasants. And they probably were no better off than peasants.

Dmochy Kudly was located only a ¼ mile north of Dmochy Wochy. It had a large forest to the north and a small forest to the south of the homes in the village. The road to Dmochy Wochy was on the east side of the village and Leopold's five acres of farm fields was on the east side of this road. The fields for the other two families in the village were located to the west and south of the village homes.

My great-grandfather Leopold Zuchowski was born in 1849 in Dmochy Wochy and was the youngest and seventh child in his family. His prospects of owning a farm were very small. His marriage to Anna Dmochowska changed his prospects. Anna was born in Dmochy Kudly in 1851 and was the oldest daughter of a Klemens Dmochowski and Marianna Zaluska. Klemens was a farmer in the next village and did not have a son. Anna and Leopold were married in 1875 and Leopold became the heir to Klemens Dmochowski's farm. Early Poles used the custom of *swaty* or go-betweens and this may have been the case for Leopold and Anna. Females could not inherit land and as Anna passed through her early 20's, her father sought out an eligible husband for her and a worthy heir to his land. A marriage was arranged between Leopold and Anna Dmochowska and they were married. Leopold and Anna initially lived with his family in Dmochy Wochy and this was where their first two children were born. In 1881, Anna, Leopold and their two sons moved to her father's farm so she could help her mother and Leopold could begin helping Klemens with the farm work. Anna's parents died sometime after 1885.

CHAPTER TWO:
THE ZUCHOWSKI FAMILY
AND RURAL LIFE

My grandpa's family consisted of his parents, Leopold Zuchowski and Anna Dmochowska, and their four children – Stanislaw who was born in 1877 in Dmochy Wochy, Boleslaw who was born in 1880 in Dmochy Wochy, Maryanna who was born in 1885 in Dmochy Kudly and Stefan, my grandfather, who was born in 1893 in Dmochy Kudly.

Leopold Zuchowski

Their home was small with approximately 500 square feet of space inside. It had glass windows to let the light in but at night candles and coal oil lamps were used since electricity did not come to their village until 1970. There was an electrical co-op established in the 1930s to serve Czyzew but it took another 40 years for the wires to reach Dmochy Kudly. Water was brought in from the well for cooking and washing. Wood from the nearby forest was used in the iron stove that was in the center of the home and was used for cooking and heating. The interior was finished with wood flooring with the main area large enough for cooking, eating and a small sitting area. There was one additional room where the parents slept. The children slept in a space that was above the ceiling and under the thatched roof. In the winter the children slept in the main room near the stove and the bedroom curtain was kept open to warm the parents. There was a table in the room. This was used for food preparation and eating the family meals. The two chairs and two benches were used at the table for meals and after the meals to sit and relax, sing or play games. Metal coal oil lamps were used for light in the room and had recently replaced candles. Candles were still used in the sleeping areas and to go outside. A few pictures were hung on the walls that were white-washed once a year usually before Easter.

The family had a second building about the same size of the house that served as the barn for the livestock and storage for some of the grain. There was a root cellar where they stored vegetables, fruits, jams and other foods.

Dmochy Kudly circa 1890

Family Meals
The family normally ate food that they produced on their farm unless it was a special occasion such as a holiday or a family celebration for a baptism or wedding. The food was prepared in iron kettles which were introduced in the mid 1800s replacing the clay pots that had been used for centuries. The dishes, jugs and bowls were still earthenware and the spoons were wooden. The types of foods that they ate depended on the season as vegetables

and fruits became available.

I was told by a cousin who grew up in Dmochy Kudly that a typical breakfast was "zupa mleczna" which was a porridge type meal that was a mixture of milk and cereal grains. Another breakfast meal was rice with milk. The table also included homemade bread along with homemade butter and honey from the family beehives. There were also homemade jams from the raspberries or blueberries that were collected from the forest near the village. To drink there was milk from the family cow and "white coffee" which is a coffee substitute made from local grains such as rye or wheat.

Food eaten during the day was usually sandwiches with homemade bread and jams. When available, ham, sausage or other cold cuts were included in the lunch.

Various soups and a piece of meat were normally served for dinner. The typical soups were:
- mushroom soup made of various species of mushroom that had been picked from the forest
- pea or bean soup, with potato, carrot, sausage
- sour dill pickle soup with salted cucumbers and often with pork
- tomato soup with homemade noodles
- clear chicken soup with noodles was normally served on Sundays. The chicken that was served was a rooster and not a hen.

Another dinner meal that was sometimes enjoyed was potatoes (boiled or mashed) and meat.

Fish such as carp and eel were caught year round in the nearby river and the farm ponds using wicker traps (*wirski*). The fish was put on stakes and spits and were smoked. They were used as an occasional ingredient in soups and sausages.

Traditional salads on the Zuchowski dinner table were:

- *Mizeria* which was made from cucumbers in sour cream and dill
- Cole Slaw which was a blend of freshly shredded cabbage, carrots, mayonnaise and spices
- *Surówka warzywna* which is sauerkraut, apples, carrot and onion
- Pickled cucumbers

On Sundays and holidays the meals were more fancy and included dishes such as:
- *Schabowy kotlet* which was a pork tenderloin coated with breadcrumbs
- *Łowcy gulasz* (Hunters stew) which was a stew of sauerkraut and meat
- *Kotlet mielony* which was minced meat prepared with eggs, bread crumbs, garlic, and salt and pepper rolled into a ball and fried in onion butter.

Meat was not served every day and was considered a special meal by the family. If Leopold needed a cow or a pig slaughtered to make sausages, ham and other cold cuts, the butcher came to the farm. Meats were pickled, salted and dried to preserve them for storage. The Zuchowski family diet was probably healthier because most items were from their farm and homemade. Since there was no electricity in the Dmochy Kudly until 1970, the Zuchowski family used root cellars to store their food.

Childbirths

All of the Zuchowski children were born at home. Since Stefan was the youngest, he could not tell me of any of the customs surrounding this event but from accounts by other people, I believe the following may have occurred in the Zuchowski household.

Polish wives who became pregnant followed many ancient customs that they thought were needed to protect the mother and the child and ensure a safe birth and healthy child.
- The family tried to keep the pregnancies secret for as long as possible. Even after the condition of the mother became obvious, the pregnancy was not discussed in detail. They felt that this was needed to protect the mother and infant from jealousy and witchcraft.
- There were many customs that the mother followed to prevent problems with the birth and various ailments such as lameness, being cross-eyed or any deformity.
- There were also customs to aid in determining how beautiful or handsome they would be, or how happy and talkative they would be.

There were many customs that were thought to be determining factors in predicting the sex of the child. These included:
- The complexion of the mother
- The types of food the mother preferred
- Would be the same as the first person entering the house on Christmas Eve.

Most expectant mothers continued to do chores during pregnancy and ignored the pains until labor began. As the expected birth grew closer the home was prepared for the birth. A screen was put up to separate the bed from the rest of the room and the window was also covered.

In early Polish villages, older, respected women called *babka or baba* were asked to help deliver the babies. Trained midwives were unknown in rural Poland in the late 1800s. Babka helped the mother through the painful physical stages of the birth and then helped introduce the baby to the community. The babka acted as a part of the family after the birth.

In Poland, there was no set time to baptize the child after the birth. Healthy children were taken to the church and christened as early as the next day but usually within a few days. The christening of a weak or sick child may have been put off for 3 to 4 weeks waiting for the child to gain strength.

The father normally chose the name of a son and the mother was responsible for naming their daughters. Godparents could suggest a name but they could not demand it be used. Some Polish children were given the name of the saint for whom the day of birth was called. If they were given the name of another saint, that saint's day had usually passed in the calendar year. The child's name was kept secret until the christening. It was whispered to the godmother just before departing for the church. The godmother was also responsible for dressing the infant for the christening.

The baptismal records that I have found in church registers from the Russian partition are in a narrative format that begins by stating that the father brings his child to the church and then gives the names of two respected adult males who attest to the birth. The record then gives the name of the mother and the name of the infant. The godparents are named and then this is followed with the signature of the priest.

A festive meal and celebration followed the christening to welcome the infant into the Polish community. The babka made pierogi from fresh flour that had been newly grounded from grain that the father had given to the miller. If a family could afford it, pig or chicken or goose was served. A special vodka drink called pepkowa was prepared with honey or sugar and served. Guests did not come empty handed and usually came with a variety of foods and gifts for the new infant. Some of the gifts were symbolic. A boy was given a piece of bread and a girl was given a needle. These gifts would help the boy become a successful farmer and the girl a good housewife with a plentiful supply of clothing for her family.

The most important food at the christening celebration was the ritual loaf of bread (kukielki). Folklore believed that the bigger the kukiela, the more the child would grow. The next most important food for the meal was cheese which many thought gave power to repel evil. The celebration included many hours of song, dance and music. The celebrations for the Zuchowski children lasted into the evening hours of the day of the christening. However, the celebration for a wealthy family may have lasted for a few days and up to a whole week.

An important early need in the care of the infant was rocking them in their cradles. This was the responsibility of the entire family but usually was done by the youngest child. Elderly grandparents who could no longer work in the fields were also called upon to do this important task. Lullabies normally accompanied the rocking of the child.

There were also many practices that were followed that were thought to protect the child. Some of these practices are:
- No one was allowed to walk or jump over a child fearing that this would stunt the child's growth.
- Many preferred the first haircut to be done when the child was three years old and to be done on Holy Saturday.
- Parents listened carefully for the child to say mama or tata for the first time. It was believed that this would predict the sex of the next child to be born into the family.

Farm Chores
The farm was small with only about 5 acres (12 hectares) of tillable land. The fields were often cropped as three or four narrow strips, with each strip growing a different crop. This enabled the Zuchowski family to be self sufficient as it grew what it needed, plus it meant that the work of harvesting was spread throughout the year and not happening all at once. This system also had the advantage that if one crop failed, there was always the chance of the others succeeding. The final and most significant benefit was

that it enabled some kind of crop rotation to be undertaken and thus keep the land fertile.

Leopold planted wheat, oats and rye for grains and corn, beets potatoes, tomatoes, onions, carrots, cabbages, cucumbers and beans for vegetables. They had a dairy cow that gave the family milk and they had about a dozen chickens for their eggs and occasional chicken in the pot of stew. The most important animal that they owned was a horse that furnished the muscle to plow the fields and pull loads on the cart.

Children in rural Poland were given responsibilities and chores very early in life. The Zuchowski children started helping with the chores at as early age as possible. By 6 years old, all were contributing some effort to the daily workload. As the children grew, they were given more physically challenging chores to help with the farm work. All of the children worked hard to help their parents and Stefan told me that he did not have time to go to school.

One of the most traditional jobs given to the young Zuchowski children was tending the family cow and the flocks of chickens and geese.

The two younger children Stefan and Marianna normally did the following daily chores:
- The cow was milked twice a day; once in the morning and again in the evening.
- Eggs had to be gathered from the hens for the daily meals.
- The horse and the chickens needed to be fed.
- The gardens and fields needed to be tended by clearing any weeds that appeared in with the crops.

The older brothers Stanislaw and Bronislaw were usually assigned more physical tasks such as:
- Water had to be brought from the well for cooking and washing.
- Wood had to be brought in from the pile outside for the

cooking stove and heating the house.
- With the help of their father Leopold and the older boys felled trees and chopped them up to keep the wood pile supplied.
- They also helped their father in the fields when needed.

Beginning in the spring, the family livestock was led to the pasture by one of younger children after tending to their morning chores. This was my Stefan's main chore until he was about 13. He received a cloth bag containing some bread and cheese for his lunch and if he was still hungry after he ate this, he foraged for fruits and nuts.

As the animals grazed in the meadows and pastures, it was his job to make sure the livestock did not wander or cause any destruction. The pasture was shared by a number of families and this meant that there were a number of children watching over their parents' livestock. Watching the livestock graze in the field was a dull chore and the children became bored very quickly and this led to the children finding ways to amuse themselves.

Stefan told me that the youngest child stayed and watched the livestock while the others played games or swam in the nearby pond.

The young shepherds explored the surrounding forests and meadows. They filled their days during the long grazing season climbing trees, swimming and exploring the nearby meadows and forests. They searched for wild strawberries, blueberries and blackberries. They spent hours learning to catch toads and fish with their hands and later they also used small baskets that they made from the rushes and cattails that they found along the river bank.

On some days, the young shepherds had to spend time collecting various herbs such as wild sorrel and caraway to take home to their mothers for cooking. They also gathered nuts and mushrooms that were in the nearby forests. This task meant that they had to learn which wild plants were edible and which were not.

Other activities that the children may have enjoyed when not exploring the countryside were:
- The older boys used their knives to make whistles and windmills.
- On days when the temperature had a chill, they built a camp fire to gather around. Around the fire, they told tales that they overheard from travelers and baked potatoes that they brought from home or found in the nearby field.

They were in the meadows and pastures from early spring to the first flurries of winter.

Painting Return from Pasture (1876) by Josef Szermentowski at the National Museum in Krakow

Another important aspect of rural life in Poland was the willow tree which was very common. Its wood and bark were useful to make many items:
- The bark and roots were used for making home medicine.
- The willow shoots were used to make various baskets that were needed to carry things around the farm such as vegetables from the garden or berries from the fields.
- Dyes used in fabrics were made from the willow roots and bark.
- The Zuchowski children also enjoyed the toys that their father made from the willow wood.
- The feed for the cow was occasionally supplemented with the leaves and young shoots from the willow tree.

Daughter Marianna shared some of the chores with her brothers but eventually she was given chores in the house to help her mother with the cooking and cleaning. Initially she helped by cleaning and setting the table. Another step in her domestic training was cleaning and cutting-up vegetables that were added to the stews prepared by her mother. Learning to sew to mend clothes was also important.

As Marianna grew older she began helping her mother with the laundry which was done once a week. At first she would hang the clothes up to dry and then fold them once they were ready. As she grew taller and stronger she would aid her mother in the washing of the clothes which was very physically demanding.

Marianna and her mother placed the clothes in a tub to soak overnight. The next day they would rinse the clothes in fresh water and then placed them in a trough (called a *tryfus*) which had high legs and it had holes in the bottom. They then poured hot lye over the clothes. The lye soaked through all of the layers of the clothes and ran out the bottom holes into a tub that had been place under the trough. The lye was re-heated and poured into the trough several times until the clothes were thoroughly steamed. The women then put the clothes back into the fresh water to press out the lye. The clothes were then hung up to dry.

Starch was made from rye grain which was boiled and beaten to thicken it. When starch was used the clothes were press and put through a roller. They were then folded and placed in chests until they were used on holy days.

Planting and Harvest
In the spring, the whole family helped with the planting. Leopold hitched up the horse to the wooden plow and started turning over the fields. The children would walk behind the plow and hand spread the seeds for the various crops. As the vegetable grew the children would inspect the rows of plants and pull or cut out the weeds. Later in the year the children would help with the harvest as each crop was ready. After the vegetables were picked, the arduous job of harvesting of the grain crops began. When the boys reached their teenage years, they were taught how to use the hand scythes or sickles that were used to cut the grain crops. After the grain shafts were cut, the straw was gathered into bundles and then tied off using some of the straw. The harvesters than picked up the bundles and carried them off the field and stacked them for the threshing which was the next step.

Threshing was needed to loosen the edible part of grain from the scaly, inedible chaff that surrounds it. Leopold and the older boys hand threshed the stalks by beating the grain using a flail on a hard floor. Hand threshing was laborious and yielded a bushel of wheat for about an hour of work.

The next step in the grain harvesting process was winnowing which separates the chafe from the grain. In its simplest form it involves throwing the mixture into the air so that the wind blows away the lighter chaff, while the heavier grains fall back down for recovery. Leopold and the boys used shovels to toss the grain.

After the grain was removed from the chafe, it was taken to the miller to be ground into flour or it was stored as sources of other foods for the family.

Wheat and rye flours were used for the breads and cakes that the family ate. Wheat grain was also used for the breakfast porridge while the barley was used as an important ingredient in their daily soups and stews.

The potatoes were stored and eaten during the winter with milk or gravy.

Another food that was a seasonal staple was buckwheat noodles. Buckwheat was planted in the spring because it grew very quickly and ripened in 10 to 11 weeks. This allowed the family to eat buckwheat noodles in the late spring and the summer and then harvest another crop to eat in the fall.

Buckwheat is not related to wheat nor is it a grass. It is related to sorrel, knotweed, and rhubarb and it is cultivated for its grain-like seeds. It is used as a cover crop.

Special meats such as ham was purchased only for the holidays and celebrations and lamb was purchased in the autumn as part of the fall harvest celebration.

Oats were the major source for the feed given to the livestock. It was probably planted in one of the strips in the spring for an autumn harvest. It could also be planted in another strip in the autumn for harvest in the late summer of next year.

A by-product of the wheat harvest was the straw that was left after separating the seeds. It could be used as a construction material for roofing thatch. This gave a fresh source for repairing or replacing older sections.

Once a week the farmers gathered in Czyzew to buy and sell excess grain and vegetables. Livestock sales took place only at the fairs. This happened in the square next to Saint Peter and Paul's Catholic Church.

Memories of Dziadka

Czyzew Market circa 1880

Czyzew was the center of commerce for the area and that is where the Catholic Church was located on land donated by a local Catholic lord. However, in 1900 the majority of the population of the town was the families of the Jewish merchants. In 1897 the population was listed at 1785 with 1596 Jewish and 189 Christians. The rural population surrounding Czyzew was Roman Catholic.

There were about 30 to 40 non-Jewish families living in Czyzew. These were the community officials, post office, police, teachers, private tutors, doctors, an apothecary, storekeepers, a baker, a wine tavern and priests.

Jewish commerce encompassed all possible and necessary goods and services. There were artisans who made goods for local consumption and for export to the cities such as Moscow and Warsaw. Some Jewish religious goods were also exported to America. There were two iron stores, two wood warehouses, two shoe businesses and two wholesalers of building materials. There were small food stores, fancy and dry goods stores, grain traders and horse dealers.

Leopold's death

Leopold died in 1906 at age 57. His death caused a major change in the lives of the Zuchowski children. No longer did they have their father directing and overseeing their efforts. It also signaled the beginning of a new phase in each of the children's lives. Title to the farm passed to oldest son Stanislaw and his siblings had to look seriously at what they needed to do to depart the home that they had known for all of the young lives. Leopold's wife Anna lived with her son Stanislaw until she died sometime before 1910. Son Boleslaw quickly decided to leave Dmochy for America in 1907. Daughter Marianna married in 1906 but lived with her brothers and mother until after her mother had died. Son Stefan was too young to leave with Boleslaw and stayed to help Stanislaw but left in 1912 after Stanislaw married and he had reached the age of 19.

Death Customs

As Leopold was dying, the family said prayers and recited litanies asking God to help their father overcome his illness. The priest from nearby Czyzew was brought to the house for him to hear Leopold's confession and to give him the last sacraments. A scapular was place around his neck to protect him and a candle called a *gromica* was placed in his hands. This candle had been blessed at the Feast of Purification and was hoped to give additional protection and peace.

Another custom that was followed was to have the church bells rung. These were bells that hung on the outside of the church and were not the main bells in the church tower. This practice was called *dzwonki za konajacych* and the sound of these bells were a request to the villagers to pray for the Leopold and ask god to be merciful and release him from his misery.

When death came, the Leopold was placed on a wood plank that had been placed between two chairs. The body remained on the plank for three days where it was cleaned and dressed for burial. The body was washed with hot water and herbs. The women, who were washing the body, sang hymns as part of this Polish tradition.

Memories of Dziadka

Early death customs called for the body to be dressed in a death shirt that was called a *koszula śmiertelna.* In sewing this shirt, care was taken to avoid knots. The Poles feared that the departed would return and demand that they be redressed because their sins were trapped within the knots. The needle that was used to sew the shirt was left in the shirt. All leftover cloth was destroyed to prevent harm to anyone. The death shirt was long and reached down to the ankles. Adult males had a black ribbon wrapped around their waist, neck and wrists.

By the time Leopold died, the death shirt was replaced with dressing the person in their Sunday best clothes. Leopold was probably dressed a black suit and a hat for his burial. It was also the custom for Leopold's body to be buried wearing his boots. His wife Anna was expected to have prepared an entire outfit for herself and Leopold while she was still in good health.

Leopold's body was placed in the coffin on the day of burial. His coffin was made from plain wood using the wood from a pine tree. Clear wood without knots was used. The coffin was made with wood pegs instead of metal nails. It was left unpainted except for a black cross in the middle of the lid. The top corners had written "in the name of Jesus." The bottom corners had "Heart of Mary."

The coffin was removed from the house feet first. The pallbearers bumped the sides of the coffin against the doorway three times as a means for Leopold to say goodbye to his home for the final time. After his coffin had passed over the threshold water was poured on the ground behind the coffin as a symbol to prevent the soul from returning.

Neighbors and friends joined the funeral procession behind the coffin as it was carried towards the cemetery. However, before they arrived at the cemetery, it stopped and prayers were said asking for forgiveness for any transgression that the Leopold may have committed against them. Most of those in procession turned around and went home. The immediate family then proceeded to the cemetery with the coffin for the burial. The grave was marked with a wood cross that was made from birch and it had the name of the deceased inscribed on it.

After the burial, the family returned home for a gathering of family and friends that also included the traditional Polish food.

Zuchowski Marriages
With the death of his father, it was now the responsibility of Stanislaw to find a husband for Marianna and to find a szlachta wife for himself. He probably helped Boleslaw immigrate to America and let Stefan work on the farm until it was time for him to set out on his own.

It should be noted that Mariana's marriage in Dmochy was after her father's death and may have been at a younger age due to the early death of her father. Marianna married Wicenty Łapiński in 1906 at age 19 this was shortly before he left for America in September 1906. Wicenty was nine years older and was from a neighboring village. Luckily Marianna's mother was still alive to aid with the wedding preparations and help Stanislaw oversee the wedding feast.

Wicenty found work as a coal miner first in Pennsylvania and than in Illinois. Marianna remained in Poland and lived with her family until her mother died. She left Dmochy to join her husband in September 1910 and listed that she left her brother Stanislaw. The passenger manifest listed that she was married but she used her family name of Zuchowska on the manifest.

Marianna and Wicenty had six children in Bloomington, Illinois before they returned to Poland sometime after 1920. Son Chester was born in Poland after they returned. Wicenty, daughter Helen and son Michael return to Bloomington separately in 1929 and 1938. Marianna and her daughters Regina and Anna returned to Bloomington in 1962. Youngest son Chester remained in Poland.

Stanislaw married Wladyslawa Dekutowska on February 4, 1911. They had four sons. – Kazimierz, Stefan, Henryk and Wacek.

Descendants of Kazimierz and Stefan still live in Dmochy and work the same land that their grandfather Stanislaw inherited. Henryk moved to Warsaw and his grandson emigrated and now lives in Virginia. Wacek was caught up in the turmoil surrounding World War II and died while a POW of the German Army. Stanislaw died in 1933 at the age of 56.

Stanislaw's wife Wladyslawa Zochowska (center) with their sons Kazimierz and his wife Lucyna holding their son Tadeusz Stefan with his wife Stanislawa holding their daughter Barbara Picture was taken about 1945

Leopold's death also affected the status of his sons Boleslaw and Stefan. After his death the ownership of the farmed passed to eldest son Stanislaw and eventually there would be no room or job for the two other sons on the farm.

Boleslaw was the first to leave and immigrated to America in 1907. Stefan was only 14 and too young to accompany his brother. He left five years later in 1912 to join Boleslaw in Bloomington, Illinois. Both Boleslaw and Stefan married after their arrival in Bloomington.

Boleslaw married Bernice Uszcienski in 1909. He returned to Poland after WW I with enough money to buy a farm in his homeland.

Stefan worked as a coal miner after he arrived in Bloomington and joined the U.S. Army in 1917 during WW I. He later married Anna Chmielewski in 1923. They had three children. Stefan had gained work at the railroad repair shops and was able to enjoy his life in Bloomington.

Early farm wagons on display at Museum of Agriculture in Ciechanowiec Poland which is south of Czyzew

Memories of Dziadka

CHAPTER THREE:
POLISH HOLIDAYS AND CUSTOMS

Celebrating holidays and special events gave the Polish people an overall rhythm to their lives during the year. My Zuchowski family enjoyed this rhythm as the seasons and weather changed. Their extended family and neighboring villagers would come together for the celebration of the customs for the different holidays that would occur during each season. The celebrations gave them relieve from their daily work and gave them a festive time to look forward to. The following are descriptions of some of the important holidays that were celebrated in Dmochy by the Zuchowski family. Remember that many of the holidays were related to the beginning or the ending of the seasons.

Winter - Christmas
We all love Christmas because of its magical atmosphere. It is a special time, when people forget all their problems and try to be together. Christmas helps people transform themselves from the cold dark realities of winter into a better mind by enjoying the festive celebrations surrounding Christmas. Family, relatives, friends, neighbors and complete strangers become kind, friendly and generous.

Thoughts of the Christmas festivities began with the four weeks of Advent which begins the preparation for Christmas with fasting and prayer. At the start of the holiday season, the housewives in Dmochy began cleaning their homes and they began preparing those special dishes and treats such as Christmas cakes.

On Christmas Eve, the Christmas trees are setup in most homes but not all. Homes like the Zuchowski family in Dmochy Kudly were one of the families where the Christmas tree was especially enjoyed by their four children. The trees was hung from the ceiling and decorated with walnuts wrapped in silver and gold foil, bright red apples, gingerbread in fancy shapes, and chains made of glossy colored paper. A manger was set up in the church in Czyzew and also in the Zuchowski home. The children had made many of the decorations but the manger and some of the foil decorations were ones that had been used by Anna's parents.

For the Christmas Eve Supper, straw or hay was placed under the tablecloth and was used after the meal to tell fortunes. In this farming area sheaves of each of the four principal grains were placed in the corners of the room. Another interesting custom was setting the table for an odd number of people no matter how many were actually attending.

Wigilia Table

The appearance of the first star was watched for as the signal for beginning the supper. After sighting the star, those attending the Zuchowski celebration knelt in prayer. Next, the breaking of the Christmas wafer (*opłatek)* began when it was passed to each person at the table and as each broke off a piece of the *opłatek*, holiday wishes were exchanged in the form of prayers such as God bless you, God give you happiness - *Daj Ci Boze szczescie*. The *opłatek* were unleavened wafers that were baked from pure wheat flour and water and were usually rectangular in shape and very thin. They were identical in composition to the communion wafers used in the Catholic mass. The *opłatek* at the Christmas meal was a reminder in the home of the Polish villagers The Opłatki wafers were embossed with Christmas related religious images, varying from the nativity scene, especially Virgin Mary with baby Jesus, to the Star of Bethlehem. After the wafer had been passed around the table, everyone then got to taste the traditional dishes that were prepared by Anna. Each dish followed the rule to use food from the each of the family's food sources – grains from the field, vegetables from the garden, fruit from the orchard, mushrooms and herbs from the woods and fish from the sea, river and pond. The meal included cheese, sauerkraut *pierogi*, fish in various forms, fish or mushroom soup with noodles, herring, boiled potatoes, dumplings with plums and poppy seeds, stewed prunes with lemon peel, a compote of dried fruit and poppy seed cake appear.

After supper, the candles on the tree were lit by the entire family or sometimes by only the children. Then the entire family joined in singing Christmas carols. After that, the Leopold or Anna would tell old Polish Christmas legends and different stories of how Christmas was celebrated in ancient times. One favorite story was about the belief that the farm animals spoke in human voices at midnight.

Beginning on Christmas Eve and continuing through the holidays, groups of boys from Dmochy Kudly and the two nearby villages went around singing Christmas carols for their neighbors. They usually carried a *szopka* which was a miniature stable, with figures of the Holy Family, the shepherds and the animals, mounted on a pole or a platform and carried shoulder-high. One person in the group carried the star and was called by the term *gwiazdor or the* star boy or star man. Over time, the person who carried the star became known as jolly St. Nick.

The evening's festivities ended with the family blowing out the candles and then traveling to Czyzew to attend midnight mass.

On Christmas Day, the Zuchowski family spent the day at home eating, singing and enjoying the family. On the second day of Christmas, they ventured out to visit friends and family in the neighboring villages.

New Years
The New Year's celebration like many holidays began on the evening before. In rural Poland, fortune telling was a popular activity on this evening. There were many methods practiced but all sought to foretell of future marriages, deaths, good crops and christenings. Another custom that was practiced by the young boys was to march around the fruit trees. They were trying to awaken the trees from their winter sleep by clanging pots and pans or ringing bells.

On New Year's Day, Polish people normally visited their friends and relatives for the purpose of offering their best wishes on this important day. The normal greeting was "bóg cię stykaj" which translates to "God's good graces touch you."

New Year's Day and the Twelfth Day of Christmas were important days in the winter cycle and as with many Polish holidays special breads were baked for the occasion. The ritual bread for New Year's celebration was called *nowe laki* and was baked on the evening before New Year's from rye or wheat but wheat was preferred because it gave a smoother consistency. The dough for the *nowe laki* bread loaf was worked longer than normal bread to make it denser. This made the bread harder after baking and allowed it to be made into small detail shapes. Before baking, small clumps of dough were torn off and formed into figures of farm animals, fish, fruit trees, men on horses, hunters with game and women with children. The hardness of the bread also allowed the figures to include many details.

After baking, the figures were hung from the rafters or above the stove or fireplace. They were left hanging there throughout the year unless they were needed for a sick or breeding animal. To prepare the dough figures for use, they were soaked in water and then given to these animals.

The Feast of the Three Kings or the Feast of the Epiphany

The Feast of the Three Kings was celebrated twelve days after Christmas and began the day before with the baking of a special wheat bread called *szczodraki* which was offered to visiting friends, given to poor children who came caroling and it was also distributed to the poor. The bread was shaped into various figures which included farm animals, people or a star.

During the evening before the Feast of the Three Kings, the Zuchowski family usually sat around the fireplace singing carols and waited for the carolers to stop outside their modest home. The carolers would come to the door to offer best wishes for a bountiful year and to sing special songs. The family may have seen two groups of carolers. One was the poor children of the village and the second group was the *Gwiazdory* who came dressed in special costumes to represent the three Wise Men.

The next morning the family hurried to church carrying a small box that contained resin, juniper berries, a piece of chalk and gold foil. The box was blessed by the priest and then taken home. After returning home, the *gospodarz* (Leopold – the head of the house) used the chalk to write the letters KMB separated by crosses on all the doors of the home. The letters represented the initials of the Three Wise Men – Kasper, Mechior and Baltazar. This was to protect the family from illness. Rubbing the necks of the family with the gold foil was thought to prevent sore throats and the juniper berries were burned as incense in the house and stables to add protection for the animals and family.

The Feast of the Three Kings ended the twelve days of Christmas and signaled the beginning of *zapusty* or carnival time which lasted up to Ash Wednesday.

Spring – Lent, Palm Sunday and Easter
Ash Wednesday signaled the end of *zapusty* and the beginning of the forty days of Lent. This was a solemn period of fasting and prayer.

The celebration of Easter starts with the end of Lent and the arrival of Palm Sunday. In Poland, Palm Sunday is called *Niedziela Męki Pańskiej (*the Sunday of the Lord's Passion*), Niedziela Wierzbowa (*Willow Sunday*) or Niedziela Kwietnia (*April Sunday*)*. Lacking a convenient source of palms, the Poles substituted the spring greenery that would be in blossom in their areas. In Dmochy, the villagers cut willow branches to symbolize the palm branches that were used to cover the path that Jesus took to enter Jerusalem. The villagers placed the willow branches on the floor of the church to allow the priest and villagers to walk over them to the altar during the Palm Sunday procession. After the mass, the villagers took the branches home to place in their homes, barns, and fields to encourage the good health, the production of the livestock and the protection of their homes. Leopold and Anna used branches to sprinkle the homes and outbuildings with holy water. They nailed willow branches to the main entries of the home and burnt them as incense to drive away evil spirits. Leopold and the other villagers also fastened the branches to plows, tucked them into beehives, and put them under nests.

On Holy Thursday and Good Friday eggs were colored by

daughter Marianna and the other girls and young women of the village. This was done in secrecy from the boys and men. The colored eggs were call *malowane* or *malowanki* when a single color was used. If the egg was painted with a design it was call *kraszone* or *kraszanki*. *Pisanki* was the name used for a multi-colored egg that had intricate patterns that was created by using a stylus to apply wax before they were placed in the colored dyes. The origin of eggs as an Easter custom dates back to ancient times to celebrate the beginning of spring. The egg was a symbol of fertility and served a critical role in many celebrations throughout the year in Poland. In the 1800s, the elaborately decorated and ornamental *Pisanki* eggs were given as gifts during Polish courtships.

In memory of the Passion of Christ, the family and the other villagers spent Good Friday fasting and praying in Church.

Easter Babka Cake

On Holy Saturday, Poles would go to the church with baskets full of eggs, sausages and bread, which was called the Easter Basket. The villagers would bring the Easter food to the church for the priests to bless. In the small villages such as Dmochy Kudly,

Dmochy Wochy and Dmochy Mrozy, Leopold, Anna and the other villagers met the priest at a scheduled place and time to bless their Easter food. The priest made these trips to the small villages in the parish to avoid the spoiling of the food to be used for the Easter celebration.

On Easter Sunday, families would attend mass and then race for home where they would meet their relatives for a festive breakfast. The fasting was over and blessed egg was the first food to be eaten. A slice of the egg was given to each member of the family to eat. Children believed they would get the sweets from Easter Bunny, and sometimes they looked for chocolate eggs hidden in the house. People would wish one another "Happy Easter" and would enjoy the day visiting with their friends and relatives.

Easter Monday is call **Śmigus-Dyngus** or "Wet Monday." This was a celebration that was also observed throughout Polish, Czech, Slovak and Hungarian areas. On this day, the boys threw water over girls. The girls returned the favor by throwing water on the boys the next day but many times the boys also got soaked on Dyngus Monday. Many of the girls were taken to the nearby river or pond and thrown into the water for a complete soaking and pretty girls were "watered" many times during the day. Often the girls would offer the boys a *pisanki* egg as a ransom and hoped this would save them from being soaked. The eggs were believed to be a magical charm that would bring good harvests, successful relationships and healthy childbirths.

The soakings were followed with a number of other rituals, such as reciting verses and holding door-to-door processions. In Dmochy, the boys would march through the villages and one of them would be dressed in a bear costume with a bell on his head. The costume was either a real bearskin or a bearlike costume made of pea vines. The group would collect gifts for the bear by going door to door and later they would drown the bear in a nearby stream or pond. The bear was believed to have magical powers to prevent evil, provide for a good harvest and help cure diseases.

The origins of the Dyngus celebration are uncertain, but it may date to pagan times and it was first described in writing as early as the 15th century. Some believe that the use of water represents the spring rains that are needed for a successful harvest.

Summer – Feast of Corpus Christi
The Feast of Corpus Christi is a public holiday in Poland and was celebrated in Dmochy with pomp and ceremony when Stefan was living there. It commemorated the Holy Eucharist. The feast was celebrated on the Thursday after Trinity Sunday and this usually fell in latter part of May or early June.

In Dmochy, this holiday was celebrated with the observation of three practices.

The first of these customs was the erection of four portable altars in a tent-like structure that was located away from the church. The inside of the tent was decorated with statues and holy pictures and made to resemble a small chapel.

The altars were decorated with nine small wreaths and each wreath was made from a different herb – thyme (*macierzanka*), hazel wort (*kopytnik*), stonecrop (*rozchodnik*), lady's mantle (*nawrotek*), sundew (*rosiczka*), mint (*mieta*), rue (*ruta*), daisy (*strokroc*) and periwinkle (*barwinek*). The wreaths were blessed by the priest and were hung for a week on the monstrance that held the Eucharist. The blessing begged the Lord to accept the fragrance of the offered herbs and to bless those who offered the wreaths.

The most important part of the Corpus Christi celebration was the procession. The entire parish assembled in Czyzew in their Sunday best clothes to take part in the procession. An honor guard was appointed to lead the Blessed Sacrament at the head of the procession. This group was followed by members of the trade guilds, then by the town officials, religious organizations, individuals and family groups. The purpose of the procession was to publicly proclaim and reaffirm their devotion to the Holy Eucharist. The procession began by walking around the church and the grounds and then proceeded to the small temporary chapel. The congregation stopped at each of the small altars to pray and sing in adoration of the Eucharist. These devotions took place for eight days.

After the last devotion, the birch branches were placed among the growing field crops in the belief they would protect the crops from hail. After the harvest, Leopold and the other farmers of Dmochy would place the first sheaves of grain from the field in the form of a cross on a clean floor in the barn. On top of the sheaves he would place one of the wreaths that were blessed at the Feast of Corpus Christi. All those that had helped with the harvest would make the sign of the cross and the farmer would say a pray from the gospel of St John. It was hoped that this final ceremony would help protect the harvest from disease and troublesome pests such as mice and rats.

Fall – September weddings
In the fall after the harvest was done, the field work was done and the grain was milled, the wedding ceremonies started in rural Poland and continued through the fall and winter months until the spring field work began.

Early Polish parents would arrange marriages for their children that would protect their lands and find suitable husbands for their daughters. By the early 1900s, couples could choose their spouse but the marriage process still included discussions with the family and still sought their approval. With the early deaths of her father, go-betweens may have been used to find a suitable partner for Marianna. Stanislaw may have also requested help in finding a marriage partner that was suitable and could help raise a family on the farm in Dmochy Kudly.

One other custom that may have been followed to help find Marianna find a husband and Stanislaw find a wife was *tarantowate*. Fathers could announce the desire to marry off a daughter by painting white dots on the side of the home.

It was the custom in Poland for the male to approach the family for their daughter's hand in marriage. He was usually accompanied the *swat* who did all of the talking. The initial meetings were called *wypytanie* in the Dmochy area and their purpose was to determine if the family would welcome the man's proposal. The girl could veto continuing the discussions if she did not want to marry the man. If the family refused the man's proposal, it was done in an indirect manner so as not to insult him. If however it was accepted, it caused a great celebration. The engagement was called *zaręczyny* and was considered as binding as the marriage. In fact, there was a public ceremony tying together the hands of the bride and groom the night of the engagement. The next morning the couple went to the priest for the placement of the banns of marriage. The engagement lasted for three weeks as the banns were read during mass in the parish church.

The wedding was held at the parish church of the bride and the celebration was festive with music and dancing that lasted at least two days.

The wedding day sometimes began with the musicians going to the home of the groom and playing some sad tunes for him. The groom would receive his parents' blessing, and then follow the musicians to the home of the bride.

However, in some areas the musicians would be at the bride's home playing festive tunes as the bride's friends and attendants gathered round her. The bride's friends helped by arranging her dress, hair and veil. Sometimes the older women joined in and began chanting old traditional wedding songs which admonished the bride about her duties.

After the groom had arrived, the bridal couple knelt before the bride's parents who would sprinkle the couple with holy water and give them their blessing. After the blessing, the bride would receive her symbolic farewell from her parents and relatives. At the end of the farewell speeches, the signal was given to the wedding party to line up for the march to the church. The musicians played for them as they left. During all this time tears flowed freely.

The couple used one of the family carts for the ride to the church as they got onto the cart they were showered with grains of oats and sprinkled with holy water. The cart and the horses were decorated and the musicians followed the wedding party in the festive procession to the church.

During the church ceremony, the candles on the altar were watched. The belief persisted that it was an omen of death if a candle went out - death of the bride if on her side, death of the groom if on his. A rainy day for the wedding was considered unlucky, but it was a good one if the bride wept.

The musicians were in front of the house again when the wedding party returned from church. Bread and salt were held out to the young pair by the bride's mother.

The sharing of the bread, salt and wine is an old Polish tradition. At the wedding reception, the parents of the bride and groom would greet the newly married couple with bread, which is lightly sprinkled with salt and a goblet of wine.

With the bread, the parents were hoping that their children will never be hungry. With the salt, they were reminding the couple that their life may be difficult at times, and they must learn to cope with life's struggles. With the wine, they were hoping that the couple will never thirst and wish that they have a life of good health, and good cheer and share the company of many good friends.

The parents then kissed the newly married couple as a sign of welcome, unity and love.

The wedding breakfast was then served. This was really a dinner as far as the nature and abundance of the food was concerned and with music playing all the while. A master of ceremonies or *starosta* gave serious and then mocking advice to the bridal pair.

Dancing began with the bride and groom. The bride was in for a good deal of dancing for she had to dance with every male guest. The dancing was interrupted for supper; then there was dancing again all evening. A collection was usually made for the bride and groom in lieu of gifts. The collection was to help pay the cost of the wedding and leave a comfortable nest egg.

Toward midnight of the second day of the wedding, the traditional capping ceremony was held. The bride was seated in the middle of the room and, with the guests standing in a large circle round her; one of the matrons took off her veil. In earlier times the custom consisted simply in the removal of the elaborate coiffure which was a fancy headdress.

A midnight supper was held soon after the unveiling. Dancing was resumed as soon as it was over and continued with undiminished vigor until morning. Then sleep for few hours, then dancing and feasting all of the following day. A Polish wedding was considered a real party.

What memories do you have of the holidays?
What do you remember about the holidays and your parents and grandparents?

The meaning of a holiday is drawn from a custom, a practice or a tradition that was handed down by someone who has long since died but still holds a warm place in our hearts.

CHAPTER FOUR:
REASONS TO EMIGRATE

Why did our Polish ancestors immigrate to America?

The first record of Polish people in America was in 1608. These were Polish craftsmen hired by the London Company to make glass, pitch and potash burners for the Jamestown settlement in Virginia. More Poles landed in 1619 to reinforce the manufacture the pitch and begin production of tar and resin for the repair of ships.

The next important wave of Polish immigration to the new world began with the Partitions. In 1772, 1793 and 1795, Poland was broken up and annexed into three areas to be ruled by Russia, Prussia and Austria. With the partition of 1795 Poland disappeared off the map of Europe. Russia ruled the section to the east, Austria ruled the area to the south and Prussia (as part of the German empire) ruled the area to the west. After the partitions of Poland, there was political unrest that led to a series of uprisings between 1800 and 1860 by the nobles to regain control of their country. When they lost, the Polish intellectuals and nobles immigrated to America to flee punishment for their roles against their foreign rulers. However, it has been estimated that less than 2000 Poles were part of this immigration.

The next major wave of Polish immigrants came in the late 1800s and early 1900s. Most of these immigrants left Poland for economic reasons. At that time, unemployment and poverty were widespread throughout Poland. Industrial development was slow with foreign investors reluctant to put up the capital needed for industrial development due to the past history of political uprisings.

Another important reason why Poles came to America was to

escape the domination and religious persecution by their Russian, Prussian and Austrian rulers. Russia and Prussia were especially cruel to the Poles and treated them as lower class people. Although the rulers of the partitioned Poland were initially tolerant, their treatment of the Poles changed drastically after the uprisings in the mid-1800s. New laws were enacted in the three partitions that were designed to wipe out all traces of Polish culture.

In the Prussian area:
- Poles were not allowed to speak Polish in public.
- All business was conducted in German.
- Polish speaking schools were closed and all children were taught in German.
- Poles were not allowed to print Polish newspapers,
- They were not allowed to perform traditional Polish dances or sing the Polish songs that they loved
- Catholic churches were closed.
- Poles were forced to sell their lands and their lands were then sold to Germans at bargain prices.

In the Russian area:
- The Polish people in the Russian partition also suffered due to the Russian Tsar's Russification policy which included the imposition of the Russian language, the conversion to the Orthodox Catholic religion and the levy of heavy taxes.
- Mandatory 5 to 6 years of military service.
- The petty treatment of the Poles by their Russian administrators caused a rise in Polish nationalism.

In the Austrian area:
- the Poles were allowed to practice their Catholic faith but the poverty of most of the lower class led to high levels of immigration.

These factors added to the unrest among the Polish people and their desire to emigrate for a better life.

Inheritance laws dictated that only the oldest son could receive the land and this was a major factor in increasing in Polish emigration in the late 1880s and early 1900s. If the family owned land, younger sons could not inherit the land and had no prospects of earning a living in the rural areas. The early large estates had been divided many times when each generation of nobles died. By the late 1700s, the large estates had been reduced to many small farms. At that time, inheritance laws were changed to allow only the oldest son to inherit the farm. All other children had to find other means to support themselves and their families. Daughters had to find husbands with land and sons had to find jobs. With the low level of industrial development in the northeast portion of Poland, non-farming jobs were rare and emigration was the main option.

Most of the Polish people were poor and there was no hope for them to better their lives in a partitioned Poland. The Poles knew that in America there were jobs and plenty of cheap land. Immigrants felt that they had a better chance of finding a job, putting food on the table for their family, buying land and owning a home in America. These conditions gave impetus to large-scale migrations out of Poland. In the fifty years leading up to the World War I, almost 1.5 million persons immigrated from Polish Russia to the United States.

The steamship lines were also a factor in the growth of emigration from Poland. They had recognized that they could make more profits on the voyages to North America by recruiting more immigrants to book passage. Competition between the different companies also caused improvements in accommodations on the ships. They began advertising and setup ticket agents in the villages to make it more convenient for people who had decided to leave to buy their passage.

It was not an easy decision to leave their homes. Many emigrants left but still felt that they would earn enough money to return to their home and buy a farm. Some did follow this plan. Some of those who returned were not successful earning their nest egg but were too homesick to remain away from Poland. However many Poles remained in their new lands and found ways to support their families and be relatively successful.

Stefan was affected by two factors that were the probable cause of his decision to emigrate.
1. The first factor in his decision was his mandatory service in the Russian army. At age twenty-one he would become eligible to be conscripted into the Russian army.
2. The second factor was the economic problems that people in Poland faced in the early 1900s. This was the main factor in his decision. His father had died and title to the farm had passed to his brother Stanislaw. Soon he would have to leave the farm and he had very little prospects in finding a job or a place to live.

Military service
In 1874 compulsory military service was introduced in Russia, regardless of class or religion. This requirement covered all men between the ages of 21 and 28. The service lasted six years for the Army and for the Navy it lasted seven years. Exempt were only children, employees of the railroad and sons of soldiers killed during the January Uprising. Since the number males who could be conscripted exceeded the number of recruits needed by the army, drawings were organized and only those who had their numbers drawn were conscripted.

There was a chance that Stefan would not be conscripted but if his name was chosen there was little chance that he would survive. Between 1832 and 1873, there were 309,000 recruits from the Kingdom of Poland who were conscripted into the Russian army. Seventy-five percent of these Polish recruits died. The soldiers endured terrible conditions and the Polish troops were always the ranks that were sent into battle first. They always sustained the heaviest casualties. Only twelve percent of the recruits returned to their villages after their service. The other thirteen percent stayed in Russia.

By the late 1800s and early 1900s, many young Polish men were leaving their villages to avoid their mandatory military service in the Russia army.

Inheritance, jobs and the economy

When his father died, inheritance laws gave the family farm to his oldest brother Stanislaw. For a few years, Stefan stayed on the farm and helped his brother. In 1911 Stanislaw married and had a son. It was time for Stefan to leave his brother's household.

If Stefan and the young men in the area could not own a farm, they did not have any options. The farms in the area were small and most farm owners could not afford to pay anyone to help them tend their fields. With the low level of industrial development in this area of Poland, non-farming jobs were rare. Emigration was the only option.

These factors caused Stefan to make his decision to emigrate and with the help of his brothers, he started planning to leave. He was getting ready to join the 1.5 million Poles who emigrated from the Russian partition to seek a better life in America.

Memories of Dziadka

CHAPTER FIVE: EMIGRATION AND DEPARTURE

It was not easy to immigrate to America. Those who left saw immigration to America as their only chance to make a new start in life. Freedoms there being enjoyed by friends and relatives in their new lands could only be dreams for those that stayed behind in their partitioned Polish homeland.

Not all who left their villages made it to the new lands. The journey from the Polish villages to ports of departure was long even if the emigrants could take the train. However, if they traveled by cart or walked the trek covered many days and was arduous. Some Polish emigrants had to return to their villages because they were turned back at the German border or they squandered their passage money in Hamburg and Bremen. Those that made it to the port could also be turned away because they failed their medical exams

In the early 1900s steamship tickets for America cost between $30 to $35. People had to save money for years to buy their tickets or they borrowed the money from relatives. Shipping companies competed for passengers to increase their revenues. Initially the ships used by the immigrants hauled goods such as cotton, tobacco and other raw goods from America to Europe and then the shipping lines filled their cargo holds with immigrants for the voyage back to America. When the U.S. Immigration Service placed stricter health requirements for the arriving immigrants, conditions aboard the ships improved for the immigrants.

To attract the immigrants, the shipping lines advertised in towns and villages. By 1900, most large villages in Poland had ticket agents that made it possible to book passage, purchase and prepay for all tickets to a final destination in North American. The agents were normally innkeepers but sometimes the local priest or the school teacher provided this service.

The Dmochy area was located in the Lomza district and economic problems in this district forced many to emigrate. The number of immigrants from the Lomza district ranks in the top three areas of immigration from Poland to America.

The Zuchowski Family
By 1910, Leopold and Anna Zuchowski had died and son Stanislaw had inherited the family farm. Son Stefan was seventeen and was still living with Stanislaw and helping with the farm chores. Daughter Marianna had married Wicenty Łapiński and was preparing to leave and join him in America. Son Boleslaw had emigrated in March 1907.

Boleslaw journeyed to Norwich, Connecticut to work in the textile factories with a cousin. However he had difficulty finding work and moved to Bloomington, Illinois in 1908 with the Uscienski brothers and their sister Bernice.

In early September 1910, Marianna left Dmochy Kudly to join her husband in Illinois. She purchased her steamship ticket and trains tickets from the local agent in Czyzew and boarded the train that took her first to Warsaw and then Posen, then Berlin and lastly to Hamburg. She took another train to the Hamburg port where she was processed and then boarded the ship SS Graf Waldersee on September 12, 1910.

In February 1911, his brother Stanislaw married Wladyslawa Dekutowska and their first child Kazimierz was born late that year. Suddenly, there was no room for Stefan on the farm and he made the decision to leave Poland.

However, even after deciding to emigrate, the task of leaving was still going to be difficult for Stefan. He could not take the train from Czyzew as his sister had done because he could not obtain the needed travel documents. He still had his Russian military obligation. He would be eligible to be drafted at age 21 and if conscripted he would have 6 years of military service. He would

Emigration and Departure

not be free of this threat until age 30. To leave in 1912, he had to sneak out of the village to avoid the Russian administrators knowing that he was leaving. He also had to avoid traveling by train because he could not obtain the needed travel documents.

In September 1912 after the harvest was completed, Stefan left Dmochy Kudly and followed the path of his brother Boleslaw and other young Polish men who were leaving without the proper documents. He walked the 1100 km (680 miles) from Dmochy Kudly to Bremerhaven because this was the only method that was safe. If he could travel an average 30 mile per day, it would take him 20 to 25 days to travel the distance. He also needed to sneak across the border between Russia and Germany. This was his only option to avoid the inquisitive officials who might determine what he was doing and send him back to Dmochy Kudly and certain conscription into the Russian Army.

Probable path of Stefan's hike from Dmochy Kudly to Bremerhaven

I do not know the exact route grandpa walked. He probably followed instructions that were sent back to the Polish villages by others who left to avoid military conscription. Walking west from Dmochy Kudly, Stefan might have traveled near Lipno at the western edge of Polish-Russia and near the Russian-German border. Near Lipno was the eastern edge of a forest that stretched 65 miles westward to Bromberg (now Bydgoszcz) which was over the German – Russian border. He could have easily entered the forest and spent a few days in it and then crossed the border somewhere between Osiek and Czernikowo at night where he would be hidden by the trees and the darkness.

After crossing the border he could travel to Posen and risk boarding a train to Berlin and then connect to Hanover, Bremen and Bremerhaven. However it would be safer to continue walking to Bromberg then to Stettin (now Szczecin) then to Hamburg and onto Bremen and Bremerhaven.

Once he had made the decision to emigrate, Boleslaw had sent him money for his steamship ticket and traveling money.

Bremerhaven

Once Stefan reached Bremen, he searched for the ticket office for the North German Lloyd Steamship Company. He purchased his ticket and boarded a barge that took him down the river to the harbor of Bremerhaven. Here he was processed before boarding his ship. Officials of the company first examined his ticket and then entered his name on the German manifest for the voyage. A second passenger list was compiled for U.S. immigration. The second form had the same information as the German form plus additional items such as the person they were leaving at home, their final destination, the name of the person at their destination and their place of birth. In 1890 U.S. immigration laws changed to

Emigration and Departure

implemented strict requirements on those who were admitted. The passengers were also given a medical exam to make sure they were healthy enough for admittance to the U.S and their legal documents were also checked. If they were refused entry by U.S. officials after the voyage, the steamship company had to pay for the return voyage. So careful attention was paid to the documentation and health of the immigrants before they boarded their ship.

If the immigrant arrived early for the departure date, they stayed in dormitory style housing provided by the steamship company. These were in a restricted compound in the harbor area and next to the boarding docks. The immigrants were not allowed to leave after their paperwork and medical exams were completed. They stayed in the compound and waited for their departure date.

Sleeping rooms near the Bremerhaven docks

Journey to America

At age 19, Stefan boarded the steamship SS Rhein in Bremerhaven and departed for America on October 3, 1912.

SS Rhein

The SS Rhein was built in 1899 at Hamburg by Blohm & Voss for Norddeutscher Lloyd, Bremen, Germany. Its dimensions were 501 feet in length and 58.5 feet wide. It was a member of their "Rhine" class steamships which were built to meet the special requirements of the freight and steerage passenger traffic on the Bremen - New York service. The steamers "Neckar", "Rhein" and "Main" were members of the Rhine class. The steamers were built as four-deckers with three steel decks throughout. The registered gross tonnage was about 10,200 tons and displacement about 17,700 tons. Passenger accommodations were arranged for 140 people in first class, 150 in second class and 2600 in steerage passengers when the full space of steerage was utilized for passengers. In addition to this the steamers possessed a very considerable freight capacity. All three steamers were twin-screw with double bottoms throughout and divided into 11 compartments by water-tight bulkheads reaching to the upper deck. This made them extremely safe.

The superstructures of the ships included a forecastle, a mid-ship-house with a large deck-house and a poop. All cabins on the "Rhine' class steamers, including those of the second class, were placed amidships. The steerage passengers were accommodated in the poop on both the main and lower decks.

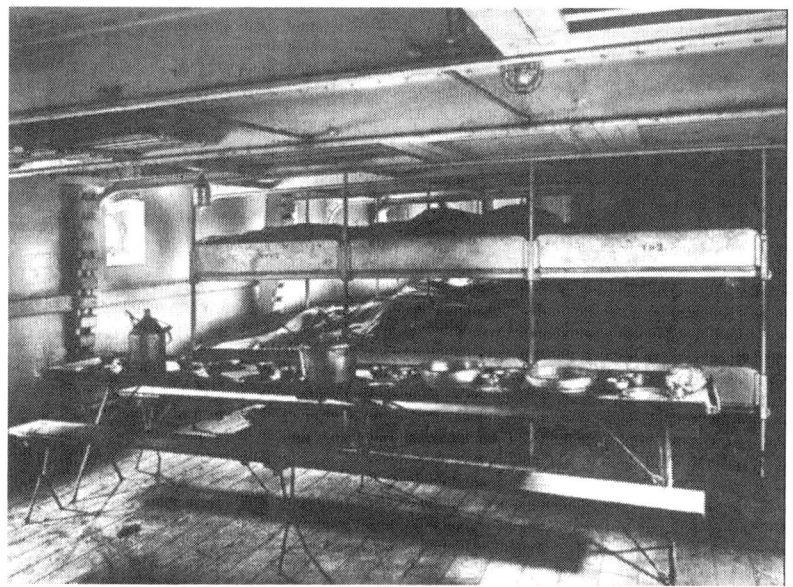

Bunks for steerage passengers similar to SS Rhein

Since the Rhine class ships could load an enormous quantity of cargo, the builders designed the handling equipment for the rapid loading and unloading of cargo. On the 4 masts there were 29 cranes that were served by 15 steam winches. The cranes had a lifting capacity from 3 to 5 tons. Further, there were 8 hatches. The crew of the steamers consisted of 140 men. The ships had two quadruple expansion engines, of 5000 indicated horse power. The speed of the vessels was about 13½ knots.

Steerage accommodations aboard ship
The steerage area of the ship was used to accommodate passengers travelling on the cheapest class of ticket. If passengers could not afford a cabin, they had to travel steerage. It was called steerage because it was in the stern of the ship, near the steering gear.

Early steerage passengers experienced very difficult conditions aboard ships. Sleeping arrangements were cramped; food was ill-prepared; sanitation poor and the air below decks was foul.

Sleeping arrangements for steerage passengers on the early voyages meant that men, women and families were placed in three different compartments that were setup with dormitory type bunks. The berths were in two tiers, with an interval of 2 feet and 6 inches of space above each. They consisted of an iron framework containing a mattress, a pillow, and a blanket. The life-preserver sometimes served as their pillow. The mattress was filled with straw or seaweed. The 30 cubic feet of space was all that the passenger could call their own. There was no space for hand luggage or hooks to hang clothing or coats. Almost everyone had some better clothes saved for disembarkation, and some wraps that are not worn all the time. These garments must either be hung about the framework of the berth or stowed somewhere in it. Nothing could be stored on the floor beneath the berth.

Dining for the old steerage passenger included tables and seating for only some of the passengers. To receive their food, steerage passengers stood in line as the stewards ladled it onto their plates. Everyone would scurry and push to be at the head of the line so that they might find a place to sit and eat after they had received their portions. Serving the food in a system of shifts would have resolved the problem of not enough seating but that was never the case. The metal plates and utensils that were used to eat were given to the passengers when they boarded and they were required to wash them between meals.

Much of the food offered to steerage passengers during the early voyages was generally fair in quality and sufficient in quantity but it was usually spoiled by being badly prepared. Bread, potatoes, and meat sometimes were leftovers from the first and second galleys and formed substantial part of the diet. Coffee was invariably bad. There were some vegetables, fruits, and pickles but were generally very inferior quality. Milk was supplied for small children

Sweeping was the only form of cleaning that was done in the living area. Sometimes the process was repeated several times a day. Sea sickness was a problem among steerage passengers because many had never experienced the sensations of an ocean voyage. The vomit from these poor souls was not cleaned up very quickly. No sick cans were furnished and there were no large receptacles for waste.

Wash rooms and lavatories were required by law and were separate for men and women. The law also stated that they shall be kept in a clean and serviceable throughout the voyage. However this provision was not followed as well as it should have been and this caused uncomfortable and unhygienic conditions. The washbasins and lavatories were made of the cheapest possible materials and were poorly maintained. There were usually too few washbasins and they were placed in a small space where overcrowding and long lines made cleanliness of the passengers was a problem. There were also not enough toilets facilities for the number of passengers in steerage. These problems added to the fact that the ventilation systems were inadequate for the number of passengers and did not get rid of the smells generated from all of these problems. The air was foul and added to the discomfort and people scurried to the limited open decks early in the morning.

Memories of Dziadka

Wash Room for Steerage Passengers

The open deck area that was available to the steerage passengers was limited. If there was a storm, people were prevented from using the unprotected open deck. The berths and the passageways were the only places where the steerage passengers could spend their time.

When Stefan sailed, the conditions associated with traveling steerage were changing. In the early 1900s, competition among the steamship companies for travelers leaving northern Europe brought about improvements that may have made Stefan's passage more comfortable.

The new arrangements for steerage gave passengers a bunk in a small cabin for 2 to 8 people. The floor space between the berths could be utilized for storage of hand baggage and on some steamships baggage could be stored at the end of the berths. There were also hooks for clothes, a seat, a mirror, and sometimes even a stationary washstand and individual towels were furnished. Openings below and above the partition walls permitted the circulation of air. Lights near the ceiling in the passageways give light in the staterooms. In some instances there was an electric bell within easy reach of both upper and lower berths which summoned a steward or stewardess in case of need. The most important thing was that the small rooms secured a greater degree of privacy and gave seclusion to families.

On most steamers some large compartments still remained. These were occupied by male passengers when traffic was heavy. As a single male, Stefan probably was assigned a bunk in the dormitory room for single male immigrants.

The new dining arrangements practiced by some of companies allowed for all passengers to be seated at tables and stewards served large pots or plates of food to each table. The passengers would serve themselves family style. Plates and utensils were supplied by the stewards at each meal and the ships staff cleaned them between meals.

Emigration and Departure

The quality of the food also improved. A typical third-class dining area under the new system included long tables that could seat 20 people. If the room could not accommodate all third class passengers in one seating then multiple settings were scheduled. The food was hearty and wholesome. Here's the menu for third-class dining on an April 14, 1912 voyage:

- **Breakfast:** *Oatmeal porridge and milk; vegetable stew; fried tripe and onions; bread and butter; marmalade; Swedish bread; tea; coffee*
- **Lunch:** *Bouillon soup; roast beef and brown gravy; green beans, boiled; potatoes; cabin biscuits; bread; prunes and rice*
- **Dinner:** *Rabbit pie; baked potatoes; bread and butter; rhubarb and ginger jam; Swedish bread; tea*

Sanitation was another important area where improvements were made. On some ships stewards were responsible for complete order in the staterooms. Roller towels and sometimes soap were provided. The basins were of the size and shape most commonly used. Many were made of porcelain and cleaned by a steward. Some were made of coarse metal and receive little care. The water-closets were of the normal construction and were convenient to use and were not difficult to maintain. Floors were now usually kept clean and dry. Objectionable odors were destroyed by disinfectants. Bath tubs and showers were provided on some ships although they usually required a fee to use.

The steerage accommodations were then more conducive to health, and those who were seasick received better attention than before.

In spite of the less crowded conditions, the air was still bad. The new sanitary procedures and facilities had rid the air of the smell of filth but the air was still heavy and oppressive. The lowest deck had the foulest air. The ventilation systems were still inadequate and could not change the air as often as it needed to be.

I have not found any accounts of what conditions were on the SS

Rhein for the 1912 voyage of Stefan Zuchowski. The ship was built in 1899 and should have been upgraded to compete for the northern European immigrants. The North German Lloyd Steamship Company could have easily improved the sleeping and dining conditions to match those of their competitors and they probably improved the quality of the toilet and washing fixtures. However, it would have been difficult for them to alleviate the crowded conditions and privacy issues in the washing and toilet facilities.

Stefan probably had better conditions on his voyage than the 1907 voyage of his brother but he still had to endure a difficult voyage. He still had to breathe heavy stale air from the inadequate ventilation system and he experienced the lack of privacy in his dormitory style sleeping accommodations. To pass the idle time during the voyage, Stefan probably found other Polish immigrants to talk to and compare stories of what they had been told to expect by previous immigrants. Visits to the open deck area would have found crowded conditions because the deck space for the steerage passengers was not proportional to the number of passengers. Also the October chilly temperatures and storms in the North Atlantic may have limited the time Stefan stayed in the fresh air on deck.

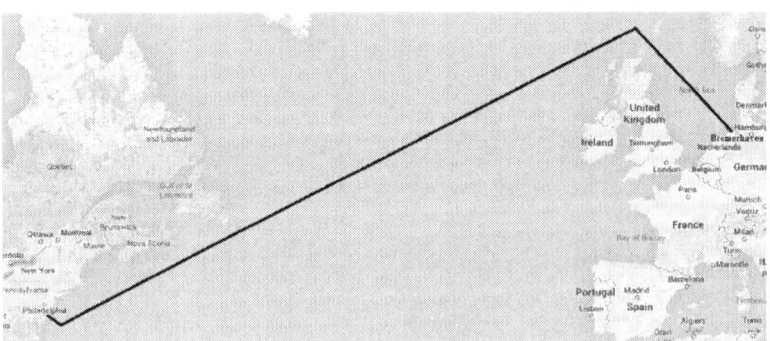

Path SS Rhein from Bremerhaven to Philadelphia

Departing Bremerhaven on October 3, 1912, the ship made its way through the Baltic sea and into the North Sea. Some ships leaving Bremerhaven made stops at Southampton, England to pickup English passengers or in Ireland to pickup Irish Passengers. However, the manifest for the SS Rhein did not include any Irish or English passengers and this seems to indicate that the ship did not make these stops and went from the North Sea into the North Atlantic and then on to the North American coast. The approximate 5000 mile voyage to the mouth of the Delaware River took 13 days as the SS Rhein could reach a speed of 13.5 knots. The manifest indicates that the ship arrived in Philadelphia on October 16.

The passenger manifest for the SS Rhein listed 960 total passengers. This was less than half the number of passengers that could have been accommodated on this ship. The low number of passengers may have been due to the cold weather that would have been expected in the North Atlantic but was probably due to the ship's company taking on more freight and using some of the steerage space for cargo.

The manifest listed that there were 18 first class passengers all of whom were citizens of the United States and with occupations of doctor, manufacturer, gardener and student. Their destinations were listed as Philadelphia, St. Louis, Brooklyn, Chicago and Charleston West Virginia. The manifest included 59 people in second class cabins. These included 11 people from the United States and immigrants from the Germany, Russia, Austria and Hungary. They had occupations of artist, butcher, clerk, cook, designer, doctor, farmer, laborer, locksmith, machinist, mason, servant, student, tailor, teacher, and weaver. The third class or steerage passengers numbered 883 people who had left their homes in Germany, Russia, Italy, Austria and Hungary. Many of those who left Russia were Jewish. The largest occupation represented in steerage was farmer; next were laborers; and then servants. The other occupations of the steerage passengers were listed as barber, butcher, carpenter, clerk, cooper, electrician, miner, molder, musician, tailor, and seamstress.

Memories of Dziadka

CHAPTER SIX:
ARRIVAL IN AMERICA

Stefan Zuchowski watched from the steerage passenger deck on the SS Rhein as it steamed up the Delaware River on the morning of October 16, 1912 on its way to the wharves in Philadelphia.

In 1912 over 50,000 passengers arrived though the Philadelphia wharves and in 1913 Philadelphia arrivals peaked at over 60,000. Overall immigrant arrivals in Philadelphia averaged about four percent of the U.S. total and Philadelphia had grown to the third most important port for immigrant arrivals.

Most steamship passengers disembarked in Philadelphia at the immigration station at Washington Avenue that was built and owned by the Pennsylvania Railroad.

Washington Avenue Immigrations Station Philadelphia 1913
Note the train tracks outside the station
(Courtesy of Philadelphia City Archives)

The railroad owned the wharves along the Delaware River in Philadelphia and built a two story facility in the 1870s to receive immigrants. Medical examinations were performed downriver at

Memories of Dziadka

Essington by the State of Pennsylvania and at Lewes, Delaware by federal officials. After the medical exams, ships proceeded to the Washington Avenue facility where customs inspections were performed on the second floor.

As immigration rates increased, the Washington Avenue building became crowded and inefficient. In 1896, the railroad expanded the capacity and modernized the whole facility which included adding electric lights and steam heating. Passengers now disembarked directly in the building's second floor for medical examinations and questioning. The first floor had a railroad ticket office, money exchange, women's dressing room, waiting room, and travel information office. As many as eight inspectors met each ship which allowed about 300 English speaking passengers or 150 non- English speaking passengers to be processed each hour.

As more shipping companies began using Philadelphia as a destination more wharves were used other than Washington Avenue. In 1912, the North German Lloyd Steamship Company landed its passengers at a wharf at Fitzwater Street which was north of Washington Avenue. The Philadelphia immigration station did not have any permanent staff at the other piers and sent staff from Washington Avenue as needed to process immigrants at these other wharves.

Stefan arrived at the Fitzwater Street wharf along the Delaware River in Philadelphia on October 16, 1912. He and his fellow passengers had been at sea on the SS Rhein for 13 days.

As the immigrants left their ship, they were greeted with commands in a strange language and fingers that sharply would point where they should go. They waited in long lines for their turn to be processed. They were exhausted by the hardships of their voyage and bewildered by the sounds and sights of their new land. For most immigrants, these hours would be the most emotional and traumatic parts of their journey because there was fear that family members could be separated if some were accepted and others rejected. The time spent in the immigration station could feel like an eternity due to this fear. If a love one was rejected, the

Arrival in America

remaining family members had to make a decision on the spot to return with their loved one or stay.

Tags were pinned to the immigrants with the numbers indicating the manifest page and line number on which their names appeared. These numbers were later used by immigration inspectors to identify the immigrants and find their information quickly.

The medical and legal examinations were conducted in an efficient but sometimes callous manner. For the medical exam, the moving line was scanned by doctors who looked for anyone that wheezed, coughed or limped. The immigrants were asked their name as a test for the deaf or dumbness. The first doctors had only a few seconds to make initial determinations looking for various diseases, disabilities or physical conditions. If any were suspected they were noted with a tell-tale chalk mark on the right shoulder of the immigrant's normally dark clothing. People thus marked were held back for further examination.

The codes in chalk were:
B – back   C – conjunctivitis   Ct – trachoma
E – eyes   F – face   Ft = feet
G – goiter   H – heart   K – hernia
L – lameness   N – neck   P – physical & lungs
Pg – pregnant   Sc – scalp & favus   S – senility
X – mental disorder

Immigrants were barred and sent back if they were diagnosed with Cholera, insanity, tuberculosis, epilepsy or physical disability.

A second group of doctors looked for contagious diseases. These were the most feared. Trachoma which was a highly contagious eye infection was unknown in the U.S. but very common in southern and eastern Europe and this caused the most rejections among the immigrants. A buttonhook was used to inspect the inner eyelid for inflammations. The "buttonhook men" were the most feared of the inspectors.

The medical inspectors bore the overall responsibility for judging the health for as many as five thousand immigrants a day. Some apprehension was well founded but most immigrants passed with a clean bill of health. The sick that were not immediately rejected were taken to a nearby medical facility where they were segregated for observation and treatment. Once they recovered they were allowed to proceed through the legal examination.

Once the immigrants had passed the medical exam, they then went to the registration clerks. Here they were asked their names and possibly over 30 additional questions. Interpreters fluent in many languages helped the inspectors ask these questions. These were designed to keep out paupers, the insane, criminals and contract workers. The questions were based on the information from the passenger manifests which had been filled out by ship's officers when the passengers boarded. After the ship arrived at its American port this paper work was given to immigration officials and used in the legal section of the immigration station to document and process of the passengers for entry. If the documents were in order and the immigrants were able to properly answer the questions asked by the immigration inspectors they were admitted.

Immigrants who failed the legal inspection were detained for a hearing before the Board of Special Inquiry. They were not entitled to a lawyer but friends and relatives could testify on behalf of the immigrants. Unescorted women and children were also detained until the arrival of a male relative or a prepaid ticket from a relative.

Many immigrants were detained for a variety of reasons. Females waited for relatives to come and pick them up. Some waited for travel funds before they could be released. Over the years about two percent of the arriving immigrants were turned back and returned to Europe. Of the 882 steerage passengers traveling with Stefan on the SS Rhein, 96 were returned to Bremerhaven.

Arrival in America

Grandpa's passenger manifest listed that:
- The SS Rhein departed Bremen on October 3, 1912
- The ship arrived in Philadelphia on October 16, 1912.
- His occupation was a farmer.
- His race was Polish
- His last residence was Dmochy Kudly, Russia
- He had left his brother Stanislaw Zuchowski in Dmochy Kudly, Czyzew, Lomza
- His final destination was Bloomington, Illinois
- His brother paid for his ticket
- He reported that he had $5 and he had not been to the U.S. before
- He listed that he was going to his brother Boleslaw Zuchowski at 1217 W Monroe St in Bloomington, Illinois
- He could read and write
- He was in good health, he was 5 foot 6 inches tall, he had brown hair with blue eyes
- His birthplace was Mochi.

Stefan passed all the exams and was granted admission to the United States. I estimated that this happened about 11:00 AM. I based this estimate on his ship arriving at the wharf in the morning about 8:00 AM and that it would take about 3 hours for the passengers to disembark and complete the medical and legal examinations and to be admitted. He and the other passengers who were admitted were then allowed to proceed to the baggage area to claim their belongings.

Stefan next had to exchange the last of his foreign currency for U.S. dollars. Grandpa then stopped at the railroad agent's desk where he purchased the railroad tickets to his final destination of Bloomington, Illinois and his brother Boleslaw.

Refurbished Pennsylvania Railroad Passenger Car

I estimate that he would have been able to board the Pennsylvania Railroad car outside of the immigration station about noon. First there was a two mile train ride from the wharf along the Delaware River to the 30th Street Station.

Inside of Refurbished Pennsylvania Railroad Passenger Car

I was able find a 1914 train guide that gave a few scheduling options for Stefan's trip to Bloomington. The best option had him boarding the Pennsylvania Railroad #33 train that was scheduled to leave Philadelphia at 4:31 PM. This train would travel west stopping at Harrisburg and then onto Penn Station in Pittsburg where it arrived at 12:16 AM.

The train then continued west with stops in the Ohio towns of Steubenville, Dennison, Coshocton, Newark and Cincinnati. The train then turned north with a stop in Indianapolis and finally arrived at Union Station in Chicago at 5:00 PM on October 17.

Great Hall at Union Station Chicago

Once he had arrived at Union Station, Stefan had to switch trains. He walked across Union Station to find the platform to board the Chicago and Alton Railroad train that would carry him southward to Bloomington, Illinois. C & A train #9 left at 6:30 PM with stops in Joliet, Dwight and Pontiac before arriving in Bloomington at 9:45 PM. If he was able to catch the #33 train in Philadelphia, his total travel time from the dock in Philadelphia to Bloomington was almost 35 hours. He had left Philadelphia on Wednesday October 16 and after traveling through the night, he arrived in Bloomington in the late evening of Thursday October 17, 1912.

Memories of Dziadka

***Chicago and Alton passenger station
in Bloomington, Illinois (also called Union Station)***

If his ship disembarked in the late morning, he probably would not have been able to catch the #33 train in Philadelphia. He would have had to wait for the Pennsylvania Railroad train #9 that was scheduled to leave at 8:50 PM on Wednesday evening. This train traveled west to Pittsburg and then through Fort Wayne, Indiana before arriving at Union Station in Chicago at 8:54 PM on Thursday evening October 17. Stefan had to wait 3 hours to board C & A train #7 that left Union Station at 11:59 PM and arrive in Bloomington at 3:20 AM early Friday morning. Since it was still dark, Stefan probably waited in the station for daylight so he could find his way as he walked to his brother's house. This second option had Stefan leaving the wharf in Philadelphia in late afternoon on Wednesday October 16 and after traveling through the night and then the entire day of Thursday October 17, he arrived in Bloomington almost 39 hours later in the early morning hours of Friday October 18.

I do not know which train Stefan was able to take but both schedules would have been very tiring and Stefan would have been very exhausted when he arrived at his brother's door. During his train ride, he probably fell asleep as his traveled through the night on its way to Chicago. Luckily both trains listed above did not require him to leave the train once he was aboard. This would have allowed him to sleep without an interruption. If he was forced to take the later train the second evening may have been more of a problem for sleeping. Daylight on Thursday October 17 would have come somewhere west of Pittsburg and Stefan probably watched the views of his new land pass by as the train traveled through Ohio and Indiana. He would have arrived in Chicago as nightfall was descending and then he had to wait 3 hours before boarding the train to Bloomington. He probably did not dare to fall asleep for this short period of waiting. He may have been able to nap during the 3 hour train ride to Bloomington with the conductor waking him up if needed. After arriving in Bloomington, he probably fell asleep in the station's waiting room as he waited for daylight and his short walk to his brother's house.

Finding food would have been another problem for Stefan once he left the ship on October 16. He did not speak English and had come from a small village where food vendors did not exist. He probably wandered around the station in Philadelphia and found a food vendor that offered sandwiches that may have been cheap enough for his small funds. He probably pointed to what he wanted and then held out some of his money to the vendor to complete his purchase. Once he boarded the train, he found young vendors called "news butchers" who sold snacks, stale sandwiches, candies and reading materials to the train passengers in the non-Pullman cars. Both the station food vendor and the "news butchers" on the train were accustomed to dealing with travelers who did not speak English. The quality of the sandwiches did not match what he enjoyed in Dmochy but the nourishment gained from the stale sandwiches allowed him to reach Bloomington.

Once he was in Bloomington and in his brother's home, his journey was over but his new life was just beginning.

Memories of Dziadka

Between 1907 and 1910, over 90% of all steerage passengers were immigrating to family or friends. Stefan's arrival in the United States was the last link in the "Chain Immigration" that took place for the Zuchowski family. Below is the timeline for the arrival of my Polish family starting with the arrival of Alex Dmochowski in 1906.

1906 – Alex Dmochowski (cousin of Boleslaw and Stefan Zuchowski)
- He arrived in Philadelphia on April 9, 1906 on SS Merion with destination of cousin J Dubinenski in Norwich, Connecticut.
- He is mentioned because he was the final destination for his cousin Boleslaw Zuchowski in 1907 and may have acted as a link between Stefan Zuchowski and his future bride Anna Chmielewska.

1907 – Boleslaw Zuchowski (my grandfather's brother)
- Departed Bremerhaven on April 9, 1907 at age 26 with his cousin Konstanty Dmochowski
- Arrived in New York April 27, 1907 with his destination listed as his cousin Alexander Dmochowski in Norwich, Connecticut
- Moved to Bloomington, Illinois in 1909 with friends from Dmochy, Wicenty and Alex Uszcienski. All three would work at the McLean County Coal Mine
- Boleslaw married Bernice Uszcienski (sister of Wicenty and Alex) in November 1909 in Bloomington.
- He was the destination for his sister Marianna (1910) and brother Stefan (1912)
- He and Bernice returned to Poland in about 1913

Arrival in America

1910 - Marianna Zuchowski (my grandfather's sister)
- Departed Hamburg September 10, 1910
- Arrived in New York on September 27, 1910 with her destination listed as her brother Boleslaw in Bloomington, Illinois.
- She and her husband Wicenty Łapiński lived at 407 N Morris Avenue in Bloomington when their first child Helen was born in 1912.
- Returned to Poland in the early 1920s but husband Wincenty, daughter Helen, and son Mike returned to America. Wincenty in 1926, Helen in 1928 and Mike in 1938.
- Marianna also returned to Bloomington in 1962 with her daughters Anna and Regina. Son Chester remained in Poland.

1912 - Stefan Zuchowski (my grandfather)
- Departed Bremerhaven in October 3, 1912
- Arrived in Philadelphia on October 16, 1912 with his destination listed as his brother Boleslaw in Bloomington, Illinois

Memories of Dziadka

CHAPTER SEVEN:
LIFE IN AMERICA

The train station for Bloomington, Illinois was a four block walk from Stefan's final destination at 1217 W Monroe Street where his brother Boleslaw, his wife Bronislawa (Bernice Uszcienski) and her brother Alex Uszcienski lived. The houses on either side of them were occupied by other Polish immigrants. Alex's brother Vincent was next door on Monroe Street with his wife and the Kopka family lived in the house behind them on Hinshaw Street. Alex would marry Helen Kopka in August 1913 and Stefan would move to the Kopka house in 1914.

During his walk to his brother's home, Stefan passed the entrance to the McLean County Coal Mine. This was where Boleslaw worked and the mine was first place where Stefan was employed in Bloomington.

The McLean County Mine operated in Bloomington between 1867 and 1927. Newspaper archives in Bloomington indicate that coal was found below the city in 1867. The same year, the McLean County Coal Company was formed by a group of businessmen that included Adlai Stevenson and the company bored the shaft that would become the main shaft for the mine.

The mine averaged 700 tons a day with a workforce of over 350 men who came from many backgrounds. There were African-American, English, French, Irish, Italian, Polish, Russian, and Swedish miners. Coal was a key factor in the growth of Bloomington because of the energy it supplied to the area's industry – especially the railroad. Bloomington coal was used by the Chicago & Alton Railroad, who ran their main line track close to the mine. The people and businesses in the region also benefited from the ready supply of coal for fuel. The coal helped develop the city's foundry industry and ran steam engines for other mechanical work. Before it closed, the Mclean County Coal Company accounted for 150,000 of 218,000 tons of coal hauled out of Mclean County.

Mules were used to haul the loads of coal out of the mine

The miners had little money and lived close to the mine so they had only a short walk to work. Members of the Stevenson family were shareholders in the mine and they erected a housing development for the miners This new houses were located south of the mine and the neighborhood aptly became known as Stevensonville.

During the winter, the miners would not see the sun for weeks. They would go into the mine in the morning before the sun came up, and they would reappear from underground after the sun went down. If the weather was cloudy or rainy on Sunday, they would not be able to see the sun for two weeks. While in the mine their only light was from the gas carbide lamp that they wore on their heads.

Miners used hand picks and drills to bore holes for explosives that loosen the coal. Stefan worked as a common laborer and earned between $1.50 and $2.00 per day clearing away the rock and loading the coal into cars that hauled the ore to the surface.

The McLean County Coal Mine halted production in 1927. The shafts were sealed and the buildings and equipment dismantled and sold for scrap. Today, there is no visible evidence of coal mining in Bloomington.

One of the last evidence of the mine to be removed was the red mountain of slag that was still seen in the 1960s but has since been leveled and is now used as a gravel storage yard.

Memories of Dziadka

405 N Hinshaw

Stefan's second residence was at 405 N. Hinshaw which was listed on his 1914 Declaration for Citizenship. This house was located around the corner from where his brother lived in 1912 on Monroe Street and it was still a short walk from the coal mine. The owner was John Kopka who was the father-in-law of Stefan's friend Alex Uszcienski. His brother Boleslaw had returned to Poland in 1913 and the Kopka family took Stefan in as a boarder.

After the United States entered World War I on April 6, 1917, Stefan enlisted in the US Army on May 11, 1917 in Chicago. Stefan listed his sister Mary Lapinska as his closest relative. Her address was listed at 1324 Holt Street in Chicago. He was initially sent to Jefferson Barracks in Missouri for classification and assignment. On May 18, 1917, he was assigned to the 6th Infantry Division, Company K, 54th regiment which was headquartered at Fort Bliss in El Paso, Texas.

Sometime in 1918, his unit was transferred to Camp Wadsworth in Spartanburg, South Carolina. This was probably in preparation for deployment to Europe. While he was there, Stefan was naturalized on June 22, 1918.

After the unit's training was completed, the regiment was deployed to Europe and Stefan sailed to Europe as a member of the American Expeditionary Force with his regiment in July 1918. He received $.25 per day more in pay due to foreign service. His pay records indicated that he received 421 days of pay before he arrived in Europe. This would indicate that he arrived in Europe in July 1918. His pay records also indicated that he received 340 days of foreign service pay. Using his last day in Europe as June 9, 1919 and subtracting 340 days, his arrival date is calculated as July 3, 1918.

Initially he attained the rifleman's classification and private 2nd class out of boot camp. In January 1918, he was promoted to artillery mech class and in August 12, 1918, he was promoted to private 1st class.

Life in America

Picture of Stefan Zuchowski from
my mother's scrapbook
Note sign by his left foot
Company K, 54th regiment

His military record listed that he participated in fighting in Varges sector from September 15, 1918 to October 12, 1918. Later, his company was assigned to troop support in Meuse Argonne offensive from November 1, 1918 to November 9, 1918. This offensive lasted from September 26, 1918 to November 11, 1918. His division was assigned a sector near the town of Vandières which was south of Metz and along the Meurthe and Moselle rivers.

The addition of the troops from the United States broke the stalemate in the trenches and the allies began to drive the German armies back in a series of successful offensives. Germany agreed to a cease fire on November 11, 1918 and the fighting was over.

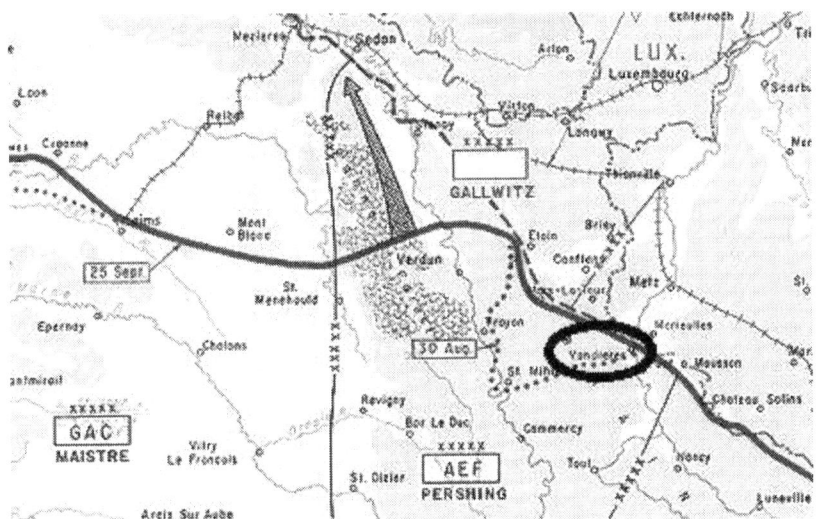

The American sector in the Meuse Argonne offensive

Stefan's military record indicates that he was not wounded but sick bay records indicated that he suffered a series of severe cases of diarrhea from November 25, 1918 to December 22, 1918. Unfortunately this was a common problem among the troops in WW I.

He sailed from Europe with the US Army on June 8, 1919 and arrived in the port of New York on June 10, 1919. After arrival, he and his regiment were processed on June 11, 1919 at Camp Mills on Long Island, New York for assignment or separation. Stefan was transferred to Camp Grant near Rockford, Illinois on June 16, 1919 and separated from the Army on June 21, 1919. His pay records indicated that he was paid for a total of 772 days of service.

For his service in World War I, he received the World War I

Life in America

Victory Medal with brass clasp for service in the Muese Argonne Defensive sector.

After returning to Bloomington from his military service, he was hired by the Chicago and Alton Railroad in their repair shops as a boilermaker's helper. The 1920 census indicated that Stefan lived with Alex and Helen Uszcienski and their five children at 1408 W Mulberry Street in Bloomington. Alex was also working at the Chicago and Alton Railroad shops as a machinist and may have helped Stefan get his job with the railroad. The fact the he had become a U.S. citizen may have also helped him in obtaining a job with the railroad.

The Boiler Making Department at the C&A shops In 1943 where Stefan Zuchowski worked

The Chicago & Alton Railroad shops was one of the key employers in Bloomington that led to the town being an important hub in Central Illinois. The C&A Railroad and the Illinois Central Railroad had reached Bloomington in the 1850s and they were vital in transporting the products from the rich farm lands of the Midwest to urban markets efficiently.

In early 1853, the C & A railroad opened a shop to repair and manufacture cars and engines as needed to keep their trains running. By 1856 over 150 people were employed there. This growth continued and was fueled by the technology being developed for steel and other materials in the manufacture of the locomotives. This meant the shops had to have the latest machinery and the best skilled workers. This brought an influx of Europeans and Americans who could adapt to and guide the fast developing railroad industry. By the 1890s the Bloomington shops had everything required to build new steam engines and cars. This eliminated the need to have parts and materials supplied from Europe.

Besides the heavy work needed on the locomotives, the C & A shops were also called upon to build many of Pullman cars. The Pullman cars were known for their advanced comfort designs. Models that were built in Bloomington included the Pullman Palace Car which was a luxury sleeping car for night travel and the Delmonico Car which was the first dining car .

The effects of the C & A shops on life in Bloomington were enormous. The shops covered forty acres and were west of the city. As work at the shops expanded, the city grew around them. In an era before the automobile, workers built homes next to the shops and walked to work. The neighborhoods expanded until they finally touched and then were included into Bloomington.

The neighborhoods where most of the workers lived eventually were referred to as the "Forty Acres" thus linking them to the C & A Shops. Most households had at least one male worker in the shops and a wife staying at home to take care of the large families. The households usually included the newly arrived friends or relatives from Europe. Although the immigrants were from many countries, the majority of workers were German, Hungarian, Irish and some Polish. Workers at the C & A shop also included many men from states throughout the United States.

After arrival, all nationalities were absorbed into the "Forty Aces" to work in the shops. The Irish families influenced the building and naming of St Patrick's church and the German Hungarians petitioned the Diocese to build St Mary's Church and assign a

Life in America

German speaking priest there. The Hungarians also opened their social club, the American Hungarian club just north of the shops. Both churches and the Hungarian club are still in use today. Families also had access to the C & A library which was located near the shops. Many small grocery stores, clothing stores, hotels, restaurants and other businesses opened within walking distance of the shops. Most of these establishments are now closed but many of the buildings are still in use. One restaurant – Beningo's is open and still drawing huge crowds. When the shops were at its peak, the morning call to work had the streets flooded with people streaming to work on foot similar to cars in rush hour traffic on today's urban highways.

Picture of the C&A Railroad shops in Bloomington
(It is a viewing looking eastward)

By 1922 the shops were the largest employer in McLean County. However, the consolidation of the railroads slowly decreased the activity in the shops until the merger with the Illinois Central Railroad closed the shops in 1977.

The railroad was considered a good place to work and it usually took a recommendation from a friend who worked there to gain employment. Each ethnic group worked to take care of their fellow "countrymen" and each dominated employment in specific work groups. An example was Alex Uszcienski and Stefan. The 1920 census listed that Alex worked at the shops as a machinist and Stefan worked there as a boiler maker's helper.

There was a diverse mix of immigrants living on the west side of Bloomington. Most were drawn to these neighbors to work in the C&A Railroad shops and the coal mines. Irish, German and Hungarian immigrants dominated the employment at the railroad shops and slowly the Poles who first worked in the coal mines gained employment in the shops. Other immigrants such as Italian, Greek and others also worked in the shops but they also owned or worked in restaurants, groceries, tailor shops and construction trades.

There were 52 Polish immigrants listed on the 1920 census living in Bloomington and 58 Polish immigrants were listed in the 1930 census records. They had the following surnames: Balcier, Barton, Bartosik, Bunkowski, Cwik, Gawron, Goldman, Gross, Grossman, Janik, Kolak, Kominowski, Kopka, Lomanski, Molek, Obrokta, Pasieka, Poleski, Radka, Rybak, Staszecki, Szymanski, Uczynski, Wrzesinski, Zaluga and Zuchowski. The Polish immigrants who at first worked in the coal mines had by 1930 obtained employment at the C&A Railroad shops or had retired or died. Among the others not working for the C&A were a shoemaker, a restaurant manager, a tailor, and a clothing store owner. One son who had been born in Poland was an attorney in 1930.

Marriage of Stefan Zuchowski
There is no oral history as to how Stefan Zuchowski and Anna Chmielewski met. One possible explanation is that they met in Camden, New Jersey while Anna was staying with her brother Hipolit at 1231 Jackson St and Stefan may have been visiting his cousin Alexander Dmochowski who lived at 1221 Thurman Street which was four blocks north from Hipolit's house. It is very probable that Hipolit and Alexander met at the Polish Social Club in their neighborhood in Camden and they became friends

Hipolit wanted to return to Poland to help build the New Republic of Poland which was formed after World War I. Census records indicated that he owned his house so he probably felt that when he sold his house he could afford to buy farm land and livestock in Poland. However, the arrival of his sister Anna delayed his return. He probably felt that he had to take care of his sister who had just arrived from Poland. This may have motivated him to find a husband for Anna. Upon hearing that Hipolit was looking for a husband for his sister, Alex Dmochowski probably invited Stefan to visit and meet Anna. (Remember that this was the same 30 hour train ride that Stefan had taken in 1912 when he had arrived from Poland.)

Stefan and Anna with the Wedding Party Joseph and Martha Zulz plus Bernadette Uszcienski

Obviously the match making worked, The marriage certificate for Stefan and Anna listed that they were married in St Patrick's Church in Bloomington Illinois on July 14 1923. The best man was fellow boiler maker Joe Zulz and the maid of honor was Joe's wife Martha. After the wedding, Stefan and Anna rented the house at 1316 W Market Street where their first child Regina was born in May 1924.

Since the wedding was in Bloomington, I believe that Anna's

brother Hipolit left to return to Poland shortly after the he had arranged the marriage. He did not attend the wedding in Bloomington. If Hipolit was in Camden at the time of the wedding, I believe the wedding would have been in Camden.

1316 W Market Street, Bloomington, Illinois (circa 2012)

On May 18, 1925, Stefan and Anna purchased the house at 1418 W Mulberry for $1100. This was where son John was born in January 1927. I found a death certificate for a third child, an infant son, who was stillborn in October 1935. The cause of death was prolapsed cord which means there was a problem with umbilical cord.

All of the family pictures taken while Stefan and Anna lived at this house show many rose bushes and trellises in the background. Anna loved flowers and was always working in her gardens when not tending to her house work.

The 1940 census listed a very diverse group of residents in the homes on the 1400 block of West Mulberry Street. Some were born in Illinois and a few were born in neighboring states. The immigrants were represented by five households with German immigrants, two with Polish born and one from Sweden. There were six households with men working at the C&A Railroad shops, three truck drivers, two janitors, one butcher, one baker, four general laborers, one factory worker, two in retail sales, one typist and the McLean County Recorder also lived on the block.

1418 W Mulberry Street, Bloomington (circa 2012)

My father told me that Stefan had purchased a Packard and he was very proud of this car. Family pictures show that the car was a 1941 Packard model 120 four door sedan and it was probably purchased new. Grandpa's pension papers indicated that his income from the railroad was $1650 for 1937 and grew to $3367 in 1947. Grandpa made the Packard the background of many family pictures from about 1941 to 1949. The car model was considered a luxury automobile and the Packard Car Company was considered a leader in technological advances and body design. A new advancement that may have been on grandpa's car were the Econo-Drive transmission that was introduced in 1939 and was a kind of overdrive. Another was the Handishift which put the gear shifter on the steering column.

Family pictures also show that the family had at least three trips to Chicago in the 1940s to visit relatives. I also remember family stories about shopping trips to Maxwell Street in Chicago. The Packard probably transported the family on these trips.

Stefan and Anna in Chicago in the Spring of 1947
Note the family Packard car on the left
and their grand-daughter in back of them.

Life in America

Another activity which Stefan used his Packard sedan was trips to Lake Bloomington for picnics and swimming.

***Stefan and Anna at Lake Bloomington
with John and Regina plus their friends
about 1942***

On November 3, 1948, Stefan and Anna purchased their next home at 1409 W Mulberry for $2800. This house was across the street from the house owned by Stefan's friend Alex Uszcienski. The purchase included two lots and the vacant one was later given to daughter Regina and her husband.

The house was two stories and was built in 1831. It also had an addition that included an indoor bathroom and a large room for the kitchen. The house had seven rooms, one bath and a basement. There was a large two car garage. A shed in back housed the chickens the family used for eggs and to eat. Most of the remaining backyard was used for my grandmother's garden of roses, vegetables, strawberries plants and blackberry bushes. There was also a cistern with a hand pump which was used to water the garden.

The top floor of the original house had two rooms and a large closet. The room to the front of the house was used as a bedroom and the other room had a couch and chairs and was used as a TV room once the TV was purchased in the early 1950s. The stairs to access the top floor were on the north side or the back wall of the original house.

House at 1409 W Mulberry Street about 1953

The bottom floor included the addition and four rooms from the original house. There were two bedrooms on the east side of the house. There was a closet between the two bedrooms that could be accessed from both rooms. There was also another closet under the stairs that was accessed from the back bedroom. The other room at the front of the house gave access to the front door and was used as a living room. The fourth room was used as a formal dining room and had an open doorway to the addition and kitchen area.

The main room of the addition was the kitchen and was very bright during the day from the windows on the back (north) and side (west) walls. The back wall had the kitchen cabinets, refrigerator, sink and gas stove. Against the west wall was my grandmother's treadle-powered Singer sewing machine which she used to make quilt squares and mend clothes. Next to the inside wall was a large table and chairs where the family of seven ate their meals. Along the east wall were two doors. One door led to the only bathroom in the house that had the standard wall-hung sink, toilet, and bathtub. The other door led to a small vestibule and the side door to the outside. As you left the kitchen through this door, you went down three steps to ground level. Next to the outside door was more steps to go down to the basement.

The basement was dug at two different times. The newer portion was accessed from the stairs and was one large room. Its floor was about 8-10 inches lower than the other section of basement and its walls went from floor to ceiling. This room had a metal utility tub with faucets and the old-style ringer washing machine. The area under the stairs had shelves and was used for storage of the jars from my grandmother's canning efforts. The other section of the basement was under the original house and may have been dug out after the house was built. Its outside walls did not go from floor to ceiling but had a two foot earthen shelf extending out from the outside wall and was about 3-4 foot off the floor. The sides and top of this shelf was covered with bricks. The middle of this section was partially divided by a similar wall with a 2 foot ledge on both sides. The east side of the section had a door that closed an area off that I believe that was initially a coal bin. Next to this small room was a huge old fashion circular furnace. It was initially fueled with coal but my father converted it to oil-fired in the early-1950s. In the winter, the open side (west) of the basement was used to hang up the clothes to dry after washing.

Stefan and Anna purchased this house as an upgrade in size from their home down the street at 1418 W Mulberry but within a year the extra room would prove useful as their daughter and her family moved in with them.

Memories of Dziadka

The backyard of the house included a two car garage and a chicken coop. Along the side of the garage were grape vines and an apple tree. Anna made apple pies with the apples. The grape vines were planted by the previous owners who probably made wine. Since my family did not make wine, we just ate the grapes. My grandmother had us pick eggs from the nests in the chicken coop and she made fried chicken and chicken soups from the chickens. In the mid-1950s, the city ordinance changed and chickens could no longer be kept within the city limits. We demolished the chicken coop about 1960.

The other half of the backyard contained my grandmother's garden. Her roses covered most of the garden but raspberry bushes and strawberry plants were also in the garden. Tomatoes, onions, cabbage, carrots, corn, green beans and other vegetables were also planted each summer to be used in the family's meals. The tomatoes were a major product for grandma's canning jars. Water for the garden was drawn from rain water that was collected in a cistern and a hand pump was used to fill buckets to water the plants.

The neighborhood had one small grocery store at 1402-04 W Market Street. It had about 2000 square feet of floor space and was owned by two butchers Frank and Henry Nierstheimer. The brothers ran two stores. Frank ran the store on Market Street and lived next door at 1406 W. Market. The meat preparation area covered about 25 percent of the floor space and as a child I watched in fascination as the butcher trimmed and packaged meat orders. Occasionally, the butcher would buy Polish sausages from a supplier to accommodate the Polish residents in the neighborhood. My grandmother initially went to this store for the food needs for the family. By the 1926, Piggly Wiggly, the Kroger and the A&P companies had opened stores in Bloomington and in the 1950s, I remember that my mother was driving my grandmother to one of these stores once per week to restock the pantry for the family meals. My grandmother still visited the neighborhood grocery to buy basic daily needs such as bread and milk and fresh meat and the occasional Polish sausage when available. By 1957, the Nierstheimer brothers had sold their store on Market Street to their store manager and butcher Donald Devary.

Stroke and Retirement
Stefan continued to work for the railroad shops until he suffered a stroke in March 1949. Work records that were in his railroad pension files listed that he was off work for eight months from March to November while recovering. He and Anna had moved to the house at 1409 West Mulberry and they finally sold the house at 1418 W Mulberry in September 1949. Stefan tried to go back to work in November 1949 but was granted a disability pension in December 1949.

I remembered my mother telling family members that grandpa had three strokes and one may have occurred in 1950. Paperwork in Stefan's military filed included a request on December 8, 1950 from the VA for information due to a medical emergency. This was probably to verify benefits so Stefan could stay at a VA hospital while he recovered from a second stroke. I remember visiting Stefan at a Veterans Hospital when I was 3 or 4 years old. I was told grandpa was very sick but I was too young to know what was happening. My research found that the nearest VA hospital to Bloomington at the time of this stroke was in LaSalle, Illinois. This was about 60 miles north of Bloomington.

After her father's first stroke, Regina and husband Marty Szabados sold their home on West Market Street and moved to 1409 West Mulberry to live with her parents. Regina with her husband and children lived on the top floor of the house while her parents and her brother used the two bedrooms on the bottom floor. My grandmother Anna cooked, kept house and cared for Stefan while Marty, Regina and John worked at Saint Joseph Hospital. This arrangement also allowed Regina to help her mother care for her father. I also remember that for a few years in the early 1950s, Anna also worked at St Joseph's Hospital in the laundry room. In the late 1950s, she again went to work and was employed in the kitchen in of Auth's Restaurant which was located one block away at 1401 ½ W Market Street.

Stefan with Anna resting on a park bench about 1955

In March 1955, Marty and Regina purchased the lot next to 1409 W Mulberry and built a new house on this lot. They then moved "next door" with their children. It is interesting that Marty and Regina never had a phone installed in their home but used the phone next door to receive and make calls. Marty ran a small wire between the two homes that operated a bell in 1409 ½ to notify us that there was a call for us. The number of rings indicated who the caller wanted. The bell could also be used to indicate an emergency.

The late 1950s saw a deterioration of Stefan's condition. He had more difficulty walking and needed to use a cane. He seemed to be aggravated more and argued more with Anna and his daughter. Looking back at what I saw he may have been in the early stages of dementia or Alzheimer's disease. If Stefan was diagnosed with this disease, it was not told to my sister and me but grandpa did suffer from some of the symptoms the last few years of his life.

Life in America

Map of Bloomington's Westside

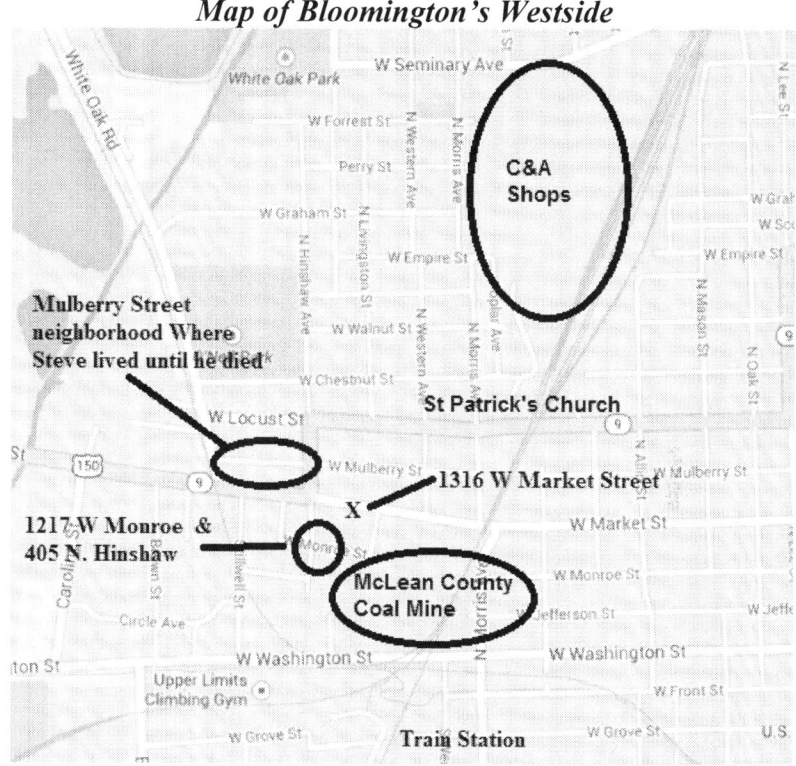

Paperwork in Stefan's military file indicates that he applied for a supplemental disability pension on December 9, 1960. *(Those eligible for a Supplemental Disability Pension included veterans with low incomes who were permanently and totally disabled, or who were age 65 and older. They may be eligible for monetary support if they had 90 days or more of active military service and at least one day of which was during a period of war. The veteran's discharge must have been honorable and the disability must not be for reasons due to the veteran's own willful misconduct. Payments were made to bring the veteran's total income, including other retirement or Social Security income, to a level set by Congress. Un-reimbursed medical expenses reduced countable income for VA purposes.)* Based on the eligibility conditions Stefan's request should have been approved but nothing was found to note the outcome of Stefan's request.

Memories of Dziadka

In 1962, Marty and Regina started construction on another new house at 103 Ruth Court which was located on the other side of Bloomington. Regina and Marty moved into their new home in late 1963 and Regina wanted her parents to move into her new home. However, Anna and Stefan delayed moving because Stefan did not want to move out of his home and away from his friends on the west side of Bloomington. During this time Regina had her children alternate staying with her parents in the evening in order to be available in case of emergencies.

Stefan finally agreed to move and Marty was going to drive him to the new house on Sunday, April 26, 1964.

About noon on Sunday, grand-daughter Geneen called her parents to say that she had called for an ambulance and that her grandfather was being taken to the hospital. Marty drove to pickup Geneen and Anna while Regina and son Stefan drove to the hospital to be with her father. Stefan Zuchowski died at the hospital shortly after Regina arrived. He died peacefully at age 70 after the hospital's chaplain had given him the last rites of the Catholic Church and he had talked briefly with Regina.

The funeral mass was held at St Patrick's Church and Stefan was buried at St Mary's Cemetery on West Washington in Bloomington.

Stefan's military file included a request from the VA for information on May 13, 1964 *(This may have been to determine eligibility for a military gravestone.)*

CHAPTER EIGHT:
CONCLUSION
WHAT DOES IT ALL MEAN?

In the previous pages, I have described my grandfather's birthplace, his life growing up in rural Poland, his decision to emigrate and his life in America. This may seem to be a biography of my grandfather but the purpose of this book was to describe the life of a Polish immigrant from his birthplace to his life in America.

Why is this important? Our immigrant ancestors were not famous people but they are more than names, dates and places on a chart. We need to write family histories that will include details of their lives and bring them to life for your children and grandchildren. Put meat back onto their bones.

My hope in writing this book is to share the information about my grandfather's life so that the details may help other Polish researchers find clues to the lives of their ancestors. I wanted to give some insight into the daily lives of the Polish people living in the rural areas northeast of Warsaw where my grandfather grew up. I felt that by tying the information to one person, the information would make a more interesting story and it would be easier to show the impact of various facets on everyone's lives.

Our ancestors were simple people. They were part of the wave of Polish emigration that left for "bread." They were forced to leave their villages and the other members of their family to seek a better life in other countries.

There were obstacles on the road from their village to the port of their departure. Then they had to prove they were worthy to board the ship and be admitted to the United States. There were challenges once they arrived to make that better life that they were seeking.

Were they successful? Did they become famous? Can you find them in the history books? Why should it matter?

I feel that my grandfather was successful in finding the better life that he was seeking when he immigrated to America. The list of his accomplishments is not great but he surpassed the limited opportunities that were available if he had stayed in Poland.

First, he was able to find work that paid him well enough to allow him to get married, own his homes, have children and support his family. These was his best achievements and he joined most immigrants in this type of success. In Poland, he would not have been able to find a job or have an occupation that would have allowed him to support a family. In the early 1900s, European farm workers earned $.58 to $.72 per week and factory workers earned $.68 to $.77 per week. In the U.S. industrial workers earned $1.05 to $1.80 per day.

Another example of the importance of finding work in America is that many immigrants returned to Poland after working in America. Some immigrants never intended to permanently leave their village. They left wives and children to go to America and find work. They would work in America during the winter months and then return to Poland to tend to their farms in the spring and summer months. Other Poles would work in America for a number of years and save their money. After they had saved an amount they felt sufficient, they would return to Poland and purchase farm land that would allow them to support a family.

Most Polish immigrants did find work and remained in their new homes in America. My grandfather was one of the ones who stayed.

Stefan Zuchowski's greatest accomplishment was his work. He did not invent anything or make a great scientific discovery. However, like most immigrants he supplied his muscle and sweat to a major

Conclusion

industry that made it possible for the United States to become the great industrial power that it was during the twentieth century.

My grandfather worked in a railroad shop that repaired and built train cars and engines. He worked in the department that worked on the powerful steam engines that pulled the freight cars. The development of the massive complex network of trains was one of the major factors for the growth of the United States.

Other immigrants had similar work experiences. Many worked in the factories that produced the goods that were needed for the growing population in the U.S. or they settled on new farms lands that became available as development moved westward across the United States.

As the U.S. became the leading industrial power in the world, the rapid growth of heavy industry had a ripple effect on other sectors of the U.S, economy – mining, heavy equipment, petroleum, manufacturing and the food industrials all saw rapid growth. This demanded more workers and the huge spike in immigration from Europe in the early 1900s gave the needed manpower.

Our immigrant ancestors were important contributors to this tremendous growth but we will not find their names on plaques or in the history books. However, we should be careful to recognize their contributions in our family history.

My grandfather's success was not easy. He could read and write but he had not attended school. Also initially he could not speak English. His educational qualification limited his jobs to those that only required muscle and a desire to work hard. His first job was in the coal mine that was in Bloomington. He probably joined the U.S. Army to escape this and receive better skills from his military service. One important skill that he received from his military training was becoming proficient with English. With his skills improved, he was able to find work at the C&A railroad after he returned from the U.S. Army. His new job still required hard work, muscle and sweat but the railroad paid more and was less dangerous than the coal mine.

He married four years after he returned from military service. He had three children and his descendants number three children, two grandchildren, seven great-grandchildren, fourteen great-great-grandchildren and nine great-great-great-grandchildren

*Stefan's two children
who survived childhood
circa 1930*

Conclusion

After Stefan was married, he rented a home but after four years his earnings from his job at the C & A Railroad shops allowed him to purchase his first home for his wife and daughter. He lived in this small home for about twenty years.

***Stefan and Anna on the porch
of the first home he owned***

The second home he purchased was over twice the size and was large enough for both of his children along with his son-in-law and grandchildren.

Stefan and Anna in front of the second house they owned

Conclusion

One of his prize possessions was the 1941 Packard 4 door sedan that he purchased new. This was a luxury car and a major upgrade from the Model T type cars that he had previously owned. He was very proud of his car and drove it as much as he could.

*__Daughter Regina and
The 1941 Packard 120 4Dr Sedan__*

Again I ask; What does it all mean? Why are the homes that Stefan purchased and his car important?

Stefan Zuchowski could only depend on his muscle and sweat to survive. He endured many challenges to leave his birthplace in Poland to build a better life in the United States. He worked hard to build a better life. His jobs required his strong back and muscles. His work in the coal mine was dangerous and dirty. His homes and luxury car gave him a sense of accomplishment for his hard work. Being with his children and grandchildren gave him enjoyment. This was the height of his accomplishments and more than what he would have had if he stayed in Poland. He had achieved the better life he sought when he emigrated from Poland.

He was not a person whose accomplishments would be in history books. However, his life is an example of a typical Polish immigrant and it may have been similar to your ancestor.

Our immigrant ancestors are the foundation of our roots in the United States. Our lives would be much different if they had not endured the challenges of emigration from Poland. Do not underestimate their contributions. They may have left us some material wealth but the most important contribution they left is their descendants and their role in the factories and farms of the United States. Their lives were building blocks in the growth of their new country and their immigration influenced our lives in the United States.

Remember that they made many sacrifices for you and helped build the United States. Try to leave something that will help your children remember them.

Hopefully what you have read in these pages has given you a few clues to expand your vision of your ancestors so you can leave their descendants with more memories of their heritage.

GLOSSARY

POLISH TERMS

akta małżenstw	marriage records
akta urodzin	birth records
akta zgonów	death records
babka	grandmother
bałtycki	Baltic
brat	brother
bratanek	nephew
bratanica	niece
chałupnik, chałupnikow	cottager, poor peasant, serf, of serfs
chłop	peasant, country fellow
choroba	disease
chrzestna, chrzestny	godparent(s)
córka	daughter
dobra	estate
dziadek	belongs to grandfather
dziadka	of grandfather
dziadunio	grandfather
dziedzic	heir, country gentleman
dzwonki za konajacych	Ringing of the bells for the dying
emigracja	emigration
folwark	manor farm
gromica	candle that was blessed at the Feast of Purification
grunt	land, property
gubernia	Russian province
Gwiazdory	Caroling group dressed as the three Wisemen
imię (imiona)	given name(s)
imigracja	immigration
koszula śmiertelna.	Death shirt
kukielki	Ritual bread for christening
las	forest, woods

Łowcy gulasz	Hunter's stew made with sauerkraut and meat
małżonka	wife
Mazovia	historical region in mid-north-eastern Poland
mielony kotlet	Fried minced meat roll
Mizeria	Salad made with cucumbers in sour cream and dill
najmlodszy	youngest
najstarszy	oldest, eldest
narodzony	born
nowe laki	ritual bread for New Year's celebration
Okolica szlachecka	a noble-owned settlement
opłata	poor peasant, crofter, gardener
opłatek	Christmas wafer
opuchlizna	father
parafia	parish
parobek	Farm worker
Pisanki	Decorated eggs usually for Easter
r. (roku)	in the year
robotnik	worker
Schabowy kotlet	Breaded pork tenderloin
siostra	sister
Słownik Geograficzny Krolestwa Polskiego	Geographical Dictionary of the Kingdom of Poland is a gazetteer for Polish villagers
służący	servant
Surówka warzywna	Salad made with sauerkraut, apples, carrot and onion
swaty	Using go-betweens to arrange a marriage
swięty	holy
szlachecki (szlachety)	noble
szlachta	nobility
szopka	crib or manger

Glossary

tarantowate	Dotting the sides of homes with white paint to announce the desire of father to marry off a daughter
urodzony	born, wellborn (noble)
wydany	military
zupa mleczna	breakfast food of cereal grain and milk

ENGLISH TERMS

Chain Immigration	Immigration to a specific place due to following someone that is known to the immigrant
Congress of Poland (1815-1919)	Portion of Poland that was controlled by Russia after the Partitions that was created in 1815 by the Congress of Vienna and gave the Polish nobles of that area a certain among of autonomy
Declaration for Citizenship	First step in naturalization process for U.S. citizenship
hectares	0.4047 acres
Kingdom of Poland (1815-1919)	Portion of Poland that was controlled by Russia after the Partitions that was created in 1815 by the Congress of Vienna and gave the Polish nobles of that area a certain among of autonomy
London Company	Group of English investors who were chartered by King James I of England to establish colonial settlements in North America
naturalization petition	Second step in naturalization process and since 1906 includes many details indentifying applicant
Packard Motor Car Company	Produced automobiles in Detroit, Michigan starting in 1899 later by the Studebaker-Packard Corporation of South Bend, Indiana until 1958
partible inheritances	the system of inheritance that distributes the estate of the deceased to all heirs

Polish partitions	A series of three partitions that took place from 1772 and 1795 that resulted in the takeover of all Polish lands by the Russian Empire, the Kingdom of Prussia and Habsburg Austria
primogeniture	the system of inheritance by the eldest son
Russification policy	Forced cultural assimilation of the Polish people that included the mandatory use of the Russian language and conversion to the Russian Orthodox Church

ENDNOTES

Chapter 1 - Farm Land in Dmochy Poland

Some of the information on the invasions into Poland based on material from John J Bukowczyk, ***A History of the Polish Americans***, Transaction Press, New Brunswick, 2008

Some of the information on the invasions into Poland based on material from Norman Davies, **God's Playground : A History Of Poland : In Two Volumes**, 2005

Information for Dmochy area and the villages were from ***Slownik Geograficzny*** by Filip Sulimierski, Bronisław Chlebowski, Władysław Walewski and others, Warsaw, multiple volumes published between 1880 and 1902

Chapter 2 - The Zuchowski Family and Rural Life

Stories about wedding customs, death customs and children playing based on information from Sophie Hodorowicz Knab, ***Polish Customs, Traditions and Folklore,*** Hippocrene Books, New York, 1999

Description of different dishes eaten in Dmochy Kudly based on information from Pawel and Cecylia Zawistowski

Stories about doing farm chores and life growing up on a farm based on information from Glen Sittig

Chapter 3- Polish Customs

Stories about Polish customs, based on information from Sophie Hodorowicz Knab, ***Polish Customs, Traditions and Folklore,*** Hippocrene Books, New York, 1999

Chapter 4 - Reasons to Emigrate
Some of the information on the travel between Polish villages and German ports based on material from ***Polish Immigrants And Industrial Chicago : Workers On The South Side, 1880-1922*** by Dominic A Pacyga, Ohio State University Press, Columbus, 1991

Information on Polish immigration based on material from John J Bukowczyk, ***A History of the Polish Americans***, Transaction Press, New Brunswick, 2008

Chapter 5 - Emmigration and Voyage
Information on the challenges of steamship travel in steerage based on material from ***Polish Immigrants And Industrial Chicago : Workers On The South Side, 1880-1922*** by Dominic A Pacyga, Ohio State University Press, Columbus, 1991

Passenger manifest information was summarized by Stephen Szabados from ***Passenger manifest SS Rhein arrival October, 1912 Philadelphia***; Original data - Philadelphia, Pennsylvania. Passenger Lists of Vessels Arriving at Philadelphia, Pennsylvania, 1883-1945. Micropublication T840. RG085. Rolls # 1-181. National Archives, Washington, D.C.; digital image, Ancestry.com (http://www.ancestry.com : accessed August 6, 2014)

Chapter 6 - Arrival in America
Description of Philadelphia immigration station based on material from M. Mark Stolarik, (editor), ***Forgotten Doors, The Other Ports of Entry to the United States,*** Balch Institute Press, Philadelphia, 1988

The information that I found for Stefan's train trip from Philadelphia to Bloomington was obtained from ***Central States Guide: Official Time Schedules*** by The Guide Publishing Company, Norwalk, Ohio, 1914

Chapter 7 - Life in America
Information on the history of the C&A Railroad shop in based on material from Greg Koos and Michael Matejka, *Bloomington's C & A shops : our lives remembered*, McLean County Historical Society, Bloomington, Illinois, 1987

Census information summarized by Stephen Szabados from *1940 Census, Bloomington, McLean County, Illinois*; Roll: T627_841; Pages: 13B, 14A, 15B; Enumeration District: 57-15.digital image, Ancestry.com (http://www.ancestry.com : accessed August 6, 2014)

Family pictures from personal albums of Stephen Szabados

Chapter 8 – Conclusion: What does it all mean
Family pictures from personal albums of Stephen Szabados

Memories of Dziadka

BIBLIOGRAPHY
More recommended reading

Daily Life in Immigrant America 1870-1920 by June Granatir Alexander, Ivan R Dee Publishing, 2009

Daily Life in Immigrant America 1870-1920 by June Granatir Alexander, Ivan R Dee Publishing, 2009

Daily Life in Immigrant America 1870-1920 by June Granatir Alexander, Ivan R Dee Publishing, 2009

Ellis Island a pictorial history by Barbara Benton, Facts on File Publications, New York, 1987

A History of the Polish Americans by John J Bukowczyk, Transaction Press, New Brunswick, 2008

Our Grandfather's Axe by Buse, Adolf and Dieter, Expresso Books, 2008

God's Playground : A History Of Poland : In Two Volumes by Norman Davies, Columbia University Press , 2005

Polish Arrivals At The Port Of Baltimore, 1880-1884 by Davis-White, Jeanne , History Press, 1994

A translation guide to 19th-century Polish-language civil-registration documents : including birth, marriage and death records by Judith R. Frazin, Jewish Genealogy Society of Illinois, 2009

The Study Of Obituaries As A Source For Polish Genealogical Research by Golembiewski, Thomas E, Polish Genealogical Society of America, 2009

Chicago's Polish Downtown (Images of America) by Victoria Granacki, Arcadia Publishing, 2004

Polish Customs, Traditions and Folklore by Sophie Hodorowicz Knab, Hippocrene Books, New York, 1999

Bloomington's C & A shops : our lives remembered by Koos, Greg and Matejka, Michael, McLean County Historical Society, Bloomington, Illinois, 1987

A Guide To Chicago And Midwestern Polish-American Genealogy by Kruski, Jason , Clearfield, 2012

Polish Immigrants And Industrial Chicago : Workers On The South Side, 1880-1922 (1991) by Pacyga, Dominic A , Ohio State University Press, Columbus, 1991

Toledo's Polonia (OH) (Images of America) by Rev. Richard Philiposki and Toledo Polish Genealogical Society, Arcadia Publishing, 2009

Forgotten Doors, The Other Ports of Entry to the United States edited by M. Mark Stolarik, Balch Institute Press, Philadelphia, 1988

Slownik Geograficzny by Filip Sulimierski, Bronisław Chlebowski, Władysław Walewski and others, Warsaw, multiple volumes published between 1880 and 1902

Ellis Island by Loreto Dennis Szucs, Ancestry Publishing, Provo, Utah, 2000

***In Their Words:** A Genealogist's Translation Guide To Polish, German, Latin, And Russian Documents. : Volume One, : Polish* by Shea, Jonathan D and William Hoffman, Language & Lineage Press, 2007

Going Home : A Guide To Polish-American Family History Research by Shea, Jonathan D , Language & Lineage Press, 2008

Polish Community of New Britain (Images of America) by Jonathan Shea and Barbara Proko, Arcadia Publishing, 2005

Polish Genealogy by Szabados, Stephen, printed by Createspace, 2013

Sto Lat : A Modern Guide To Polish Genealogy by Jensen, Cecile Wendt, Michigan Polonia, 2010

Detroit's Polonia (MI) (Images of America) by Cecile Wendt Jensen, Arcadia Publishing, 2006

The Polish Way : A Thousand-year History Of The Poles And Their Culture by Zamoyski, Adam , Franklin Watts, 1988

Memories of Dziadka

INDEX

A

American Expeditionary Force · 82

B

Birth customs · 17

C

Camp Grant · 84
Chmielewski
    Anna · 31, 88
    Hipolit · 88
Christmas wafer · 35
Connecticut
    Norwich · 76
Corpus Christi, Feast of · 42
Cossack · 8
Crimean · 7

D

Death Customs · 27
Dekutowska
    Wladyslawa · 29
Devary
    Donald · 97
Devary Grocery · 97
Dmochowski
    Alex · 76
    Anna · 5, 11, 13
    Klemens · 11
    Konstanty · 76
dzwonki za konajacych · 27

F

Feast of the Three Kings · 38
folwarks. · 9
France
    Metz · 83
    Meuse Argonne · 83
    Vandières · 83

G

Germany
    Berlin · 54
    Bremen · 54
    Bremerhaven · 55, 56, 77
    Hamburg · 54, 58, 77
    Hanover · 56
Grocers
    Devary Grocery · 97
    Great Atlantic and Pacific Grocery · 96
    Kroger Grocery · 96
    Nierstheimer Brothers · 97
    Piggly Wiggly · 96
gromica · 27
Gwiazdory · 38

H

Hunters stew · 16

I

Illinois
    Bloomington · 77
    Chicago · 73

Union Station · 73
Immigration
    medical exam · 69
Immigration station
    Fitzwater Street · 68
    Washington Avenue · 67
Indiana
    Fort Wayne · 74
    Indianapolis · 73
inheritance laws · 51

J

Jamestown · 47

K

Kopka
    John · 82
koszula śmiertelna · 28
Kotlet mielony · 16
kukielki · 19

L

Łapiński
    Wicenty · 29, 54, 77
London Company · 47
Łowcy gulasz · 16

M

Mclean County Coal Company · 80
McLean County Coal Mine · 76, 81
Mizeria · 16
Mongols · 7

N

New York
    New York · 77
news butchers · 75
Nierstheimer Brothers Grocery · 97

O

Ohio
    Cincinnati · 73
okolica szlachecka · 7
opłatek · 35

P

Packard automobile · 91
Pennsylvania
    30th Street Station · 72
    Penn Station · 73
    Philadelphia · 67, 73, 77
    Pittsburg · 75
Pennsylvania Railroad · 67
pierogi · 18
Poland
    Bromberg · 56
    Bydgoszcz · 56
    Czernikowo · 56
    Czyzew · 7, 13, 25, 34, 54
    Dmochy · 5, 7, 33
    Dmochy Kudly · 5, 6, 11, 13, 16, 36, 40, 55
    Dmochy Mrozy · 41
    Dmochy Wochy · 11, 41
    Lipno · 56
    Lomza · 54
    Mazovia · 8
    Osiek · 56
    Warsaw · 6, 54
Polish

economic problems · 50
Polish customs · 33
    births · 17
    Christmas · 33
    Christmas wafer · 35
    death · 27
    Easter · 39
    Feast of Corpus Christi · 42
    Feast of the Three Kings · 38
    marriages · 43
    opłatek · 35
    Wigilia · 35
Polish farming · 19
Polish food
    Kotlet mielony · 16
    kukiełki · 19
    Łowcy gulasz · 16
    Mizeria · 16
    pierogi · 18
    Schabowy kotlet · 16
    Surówka warzywna · 16
Polish industrial development · 47
Polish National Museum in Krakow · 22
Polish partitions · 47
    Austria · 48
    Prussia · 48
    Russia · 48
Polish-Lithuanian Commonwealth · 8
Przeclaw of **Swiercze** · 8
Pullman Car Company · 86

R

Railroad
    Chicago and Alton · 73, 80, 85, 88
    Illinois Central · 87
    Pennsylvania · 67
Rivers
    Meurthe · 83
    Moselle · 83

Russia
    Petersburg · 6
Russian army · 50
Russification policy · 48

S

Schabowy kotlet · 16
Slownik Geograficzny · 7, 10
SS Graf Waldersee · 54
SS Rhein · 58, 68
St Patrick's Church · 87, 89
Steamship Company
    North German Lloyd · 56, 68
steamship ticket
    agent · 53
    cost · 53
steerage · 59
Stevensonville · 81
Surówka warzywna · 16
Sweden · 8
Szermentowski
    Josef · 22

T

Tatar · 8

U

Union Station · 73
urodzony · 5
Uszcienski
    Alex · 87
    Bernice · 31, 79

V

Veterans Administration · 97

Virginia · 30

W

Wigilia · 35
World War II · 30

Z

Zuchowski

Boleslaw · 13, 27, 29, 30, 54, 56, 71, 76, 77, 79, 82
Henryk · 30
Kazimierz · 30
Leopold · 5, 11, 13, 54
Marianna · 27, 43, 54, 77
Stanislaw · 13, 27, 29, 30, 43, 50, 51, 54, 71
Stefan · 5, 13, 27, 31, 55, 77, 79, 88
Wacek · 30

ABOUT THE AUTHOR

Steve Szabados grew up in Central Illinois and is a retired project manager living in the Chicago Suburbs. He received a Bachelor of Science Degree from the University of Illinois in Champaign-Urbana, Illinois and a Masters in Business Administration from Northern Illinois University in DeKalb, Illinois.

He has been researching his ancestors since 2000 and has traced ancestors back to the 1600s in New England and the 1730's in Poland, Germany, Bohemia, Hungary, Slovakia and Slovenia. He has given numerous presentations to genealogical groups and libraries in Illinois, Indiana, Michigan, Missouri, Pennsylvania and Wisconsin. His mission is to share his passion for Family History with as many people as he can. He is a member of the Northwest Suburban Genealogy Society and Illinois State Genealogical Society. He is a board member of Polish Genealogical Society of America and he is a genealogy volunteer at the Arlington Heights Memorial Library. Steve also is the genealogy columnist for the Polish American Journal.

Books by Steve

Print Books

Basic Genealogy: Saving Your Family History
Find your roots! Start your search now. This book reviews a process that will help everyone start their research and it gives hints that will make your research successful.

Write Your Family History: Easy Steps to Organize, Save and Share
Writing a family history can seem to be a very challenging project for many people. However organizing your research into a format that is easily read by your family is a must. The methods discussed in this book will show the reader a simple format that will make this task much easier.

Finding Grandma's European Ancestors
Want to find your European roots? This book gives you easy steps to find where your ancestors left and tips on where to find the European records of your ancestors.

Polish Genealogy: Four Steps to Success
This book is designed to give the researcher the tools needed to research their Polish ancestors and find possible answers to the origins of their Polish heritage. The book outlines a simple process that will identify where your ancestors were born and where to find their Polish records.

Kindle eBooks

Hints for Translating Polish Genealogical Records
Quick reference guide to help the researcher translate the Polish genealogical records of their ancestors.

Deciphering the 1790-1840 U.S. Census Records: Two case studies
Census records are a snapshot of your family and finding all of these records is an important task in researching your family history. This book reviews two case studies that will give you hints on how to decipher the early U.S census which are challenging to use because they list only the head of the household.

Quick Reference to U.S. Census Records: a snapshot of the past
Census records are a snapshot of your family at the time the census was taken and contain a wealth of information that can be used the lives of your family. This book explains the information that is included in the census records and how they can be used in your family histories. The book also points to where these records can be found and also includes some search tips.

Basic Genealogy: Saving Your Family History (eBook version)
Find your roots! Start your search now. This book reviews a process that will help everyone start their research and it gives hints that will make your research successful.

Made in the USA
Lexington, KY
01 April 2017